Making Sense of Media

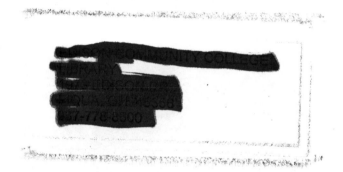

In memory of my mother, *Frances Alice Savel*,
and my father, *Simon Berger*

MAKING SENSE OF MEDIA

Key Texts in Media and Cultural Studies

Arthur Asa Berger

Blackwell
Publishing

BLACKWELL PUBLISHING
350 Main Street, Malden, MA 02148-5020, USA
108 Cowley Road, Oxford OX4 1JF, UK
550 Swanston Street, Carlton, Victoria 3053, Australia

First published 2005 by Blackwell Publishing Ltd

Library of Congress Cataloging-in-Publication Data

Berger, Arthur Asa, 1993–
Making sense of media : key texts in media and cultural studies / [edited by]
Arthur Asa Berger.
p. cm.
Includes bibliographical references and index.
ISBN 1-4051-2016-9 (hardcover : alk. paper) – ISBN 1-4051-2017-7 (pbk. : alk. paper)
1. Mass media. I. Title.
P91.25.B468 2005
302.23–dc22
2004011987

A catalogue record for this title is available from the British Library.

Set in 10.5 on 13 pt Dante
by SNP Best-set Typesetter Ltd., Hong Kong
Printed and bound in the United Kingdom
by MPG Books Ltd, Bodmin, Cornwall

The publisher's policy is to use permanent paper from mills that operate a sustainable
forestry policy, and which has been manufactured from pulp processed using acid-free and
elementary chlorine-free practices. Furthermore, the publisher ensures that the text paper
and cover board used have met acceptable environmental accreditation standards.

For further information on
Blackwell Publishing, visit our website:
http://www.blackwellpublishing.com

Contents

Acknowledgments

I would like to thank my editor, Jayne Fargnoli, for suggesting I write this book and for her encouragement and help as I progressed with it. I also would like to express my appreciation to all the others at Blackwell who were involved in publishing this book. Some material in the book has been revised and adapted from writings in other works.

Copyright Material

The author and publisher gratefully acknowledge the permission granted to reproduce the copyright material in this book:

P. 89: Still from the "1984" advertisement for the Apple Mac is © by Apple Computer, Inc. and is reprinted with permission. All rights reserved. Apple® and the Apple logo are registered trademarks of Apple Computer, Inc.

P. 135: The front page from *The Financial Times*, November 15, 2002. Reprinted with permission.

Acknowledgments

Introduction

The Media in Our Lives

This book explains, in an accessible manner, a number of ideas and concepts that will help readers make sense of the mass media and the texts they carry. These ideas are taken from what I (and many others who write about the media) consider to be seminal, canonical, classic, or "key" texts that critics and scholars of all persuasions use in analyzing media and contemporary culture.

I have, so to speak, rounded up a number of "the usual suspects" (such as Roland Barthes, Marshall McLuhan, and Mikhail Bakhtin) and will discuss one of their books that I feel has material of interest and utility to readers. Many of these books are not on media per se, but they all contain ideas and theories that can be, and frequently have been, applied to media by scholars in various disciplines.

In each case, I selected books that contain material – ideas and insights – I consider to be important for readers interested in understanding and interpreting what is often called mass-mediated culture. The purpose of this book is to provide readers with a repertoire of ideas and concepts that they can call upon when dealing with media and mass-mediated texts. Since the media transmit *texts*, my focus will be on texts that media carry rather than just talking about the media in general. I will use the term "text" as it is traditionally used in scholarly discourse – to stand for films, television shows, songs, advertisements, and other works found in the mass media. Scholars use the term "text" for two reasons: to serve as a shorthand device that enables them to avoid having to keep repeating whatever work or works they are dealing with and also to suggest that these works, like textbooks, need to be "read," that is, to be studied carefully.

My Theory of Teaching

There are an enormous number of books that deal with the media from every perspective one might think of. There are edited readers full of articles on the media. There are dictionaries of key concepts. There are books with analyses made from different disciplinary and ideological points of view. But there are few books that I know of that do what this book does: discuss the "key texts" that form the foundation for most media criticism and analysis and, in addition, apply insights from these texts to various aspects of popular culture and the mass media. My goal, then, is to do two things:

1. To provide you, my readers, with a familiarity with some seminal or foundational works and some of the most important concepts in these works that you can use in making sense of the media, popular culture, and everyday life.
2. To show how these concepts and ideas can be used or applied to a variety of texts and topics related to the media.

Thus, after I have discussed some ideas in an important book, I have a section in which I apply insights in that book to something of interest. You will find that I cover a lot of different topics in these applications – everything from romantic ballads ("It's all in the game") and singers (Madonna, Tina Turner) to comics strips (Krazy Kat), jokes (about Radio Erevan), video games (Pac-Man and Space Invaders), films (*Rashomon*), and the "1984" Macintosh commercial.

Design of the Book

This book consists of nineteen short chapters, generally between six and eight pages long. Each of these chapters is devoted to some of the more important ideas found in what I consider to be a key or seminal book in media analysis and cultural studies. I will offer a quotation either about the author or the book, or a quotation from the book to start off each chapter. Next, I will discuss and explain some of the more important ideas found in the book, and then I will show how they can be applied. I will make liberal use of quotations to show the style of the authors and the way they stated their ideas and, in many cases, relevant quotations from other authors as well. I should add that my theory of teaching is to give readers ideas, concepts, methods, insights, and the like that will enable them to make their own analyses of media rather than offering articles that do this for them.

What you will find, when you read this book, is a number of interesting ideas and concepts that will, if I am successful, empower you to make your own analyses and interpretations of media, popular culture, and everyday life. This is not an anthology or a reader – a book full of articles or selections from books by writers and scholars with their interpretations of texts and speculations about media. It is, instead, a book in which I discuss ideas about the media that will empower you to make your own analyses. To help you do this, as I mentioned earlier, I will apply the concepts I discuss – sometimes in a whimsical manner – to help make sense of various aspects of media and popular culture, so that you can see their utility.

Media Immersion and Its Consequences

We spend an incredible amount of time using media. From the moment we get up in the morning until we go to bed in the evening, we listen to the radio, watch television programs, play video games, read newspapers, magazines, and books, play CDs, and send e-mail to our friends. The statistics on media use are simply incredible. If you are a typical American, you spend at the very least:

around 4 hours a day watching television,
around 1 hour a day listening to the radio and Cds,
around 1 hour a day reading books, newspapers and magazines,

to which we must add time for all the other things we do that involve media. It has been found that children spend something like 40 hours a week involved with media or one kind or another . . . that is, the equivalent of a full work week with the media. I've seen a statistic that argues the typical American spends 9.2 hours a day involved with one medium or another.

We may ask ourselves, "So what? What difference does it make?" My answer is that all of us who use the media should be more aware of what the media might be doing to us. We use the media for our own purposes, but we must also be aware of how the media use us. The media help shape our social institutions, our political order, and our culture, which means the media, directly and indirectly, play an important role in socializing and enculturating us (giving people culture – that is, values, beliefs, and ideas about how to live).

Let me offer an insight from the French sociologist Emile Durkheim. Durkheim pointed out that there is a dual process that goes on as far as individuals and society are concerned. *We are in society and, though we may not be aware of this all the time, society is in us.* By this he meant that as we grow up in a society, we learn certain values, beliefs, and practices that affect us in profound ways. We learn a language (or several languages), we learn what's good to eat, we learn what life is all about, we learn all kinds of other things that profoundly shape our lives. This process is called socialization by sociologists and enculturation by anthropologists.

Defining Media

A *medium* can be defined as a means of sending or communicating messages, information, or texts of one kind or another, from one person to another or, in the case of the mass media, to many people. *Media* is the plural of the term medium. Media communicate texts for the most part. For example, speech is a medium we use in conversations with one another; it is a personal medium. The mass media are generally held to include books and other kinds of printed works, radio, film, television, CDs and DVDs, and the Internet. With the mass media, large numbers of people are involved as audiences in the communication process.

There are many different ways of classifying media. Some scholars classify media according to whether they are electronic or print media. Others make a place for visual media. But however you wish to classify media, there is no doubt that we spend a great deal of time, every day, using media – and, some would say, allowing media to use us!

Consider the following: Approximately 70 percent of newspapers and magazine space is devoted to advertising, and radio and television devote an enormous amount of time – sometimes as much as a third of an hour – to playing commercials. The average situation comedy lasts 22 minutes; the remaining eight minutes is for commercials. The news show *Sixty Minutes* has only 42 minutes of noncommercial content in it. As many commentators have pointed out, the purpose of television shows – as far as the television industry and advertisers are concerned –is to deliver audiences to advertisers. The obsession radio and television stations have with obtaining money from advertising helps shape programming. The same applies to all media.

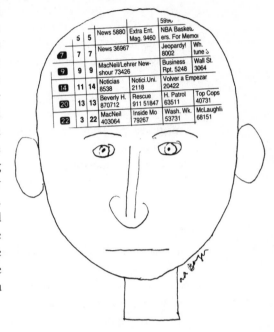

One question that has dominated the work of scholars involved with studying the media is: How do the media effect us, our families, our friends, and our societies? Do the media flow off our backs like water off the backs of ducks – that is, are the effects of our exposure to the media short-lasting and trivial, or do the media have profound and lingering effects upon us – effects that we may not necessarily recognize but which, nevertheless, may shape our ideas and behavior in important ways? There are many theories about how the media affect children. I offer one hypothesis (a guess) that I'd like you to consider.

A Hypothesis on the Impact of Television that is Too Adult for Children

Let me offer here a hypothesis I developed a number of years ago that deals with the impact television may be having on some children. It is what I call the theory of "Vicious Cycles." I took my cue from a passage in Julius E. Heuscher's *A Psychiatric Study of Myths and Fairy Tales*. In this book Heuscher, a psychiatrist, writes (1967: 325):

> The child who is being presented with an over-abundance of adult-life conflicts and desires and who thereby is being pushed toward grownup ideas, tends to become afraid of growing up and is therefore stunted in his maturation process.

I asked myself whether television might have a role in the development of some children who were exposed to adult conflicts on television that were too difficult for them to deal with.

1. Young children, when they watch television, are often exposed to material that deals with matters involving conflicts and sexuality that is too adult for them and that deeply troubles them. They would not be exposed to such material in books because it would be too difficult for them to read this material. As a result of this television viewing, they develop a fear of becoming adults which they see as being involved in adult conflicts about money, relationships, sexuality, and so on.

2. This fear that these children develop leads, in turn, to their incapacity, when they are older, to have and to sustain satisfactory emotional relationships. They are "stunted" in the maturation process.

3. This inability to have satisfactory adult relationships leads to such behaviors as an incapacity to have strong feelings, fear of sustained relationships, fear of marriage, and to nonrelational sex.

4. These behaviors are unsatisfying to adults, leading to anxiety and various kinds of escapism, such as television viewing and drugs to obtain "relief."

5. It turns out then that television viewing becomes, for many people, a kind of electronic narcotic upon which they become dependent, in an effort to escape from their sense of imprisonment within themselves. However, while television viewing may provide temporary relief for these people, it also reinforces unconscious childhood fears that are still with them. Thus it helps create the very dependencies that television viewers use it to escape from, making people, in a sense, "prisoners" of their television sets and, ultimately, prisoners of themselves.

This hypothesis might help explain why so many people are addicts "hooked" on television and spend so many hours a day watching it. I offer it as something to think about relative to the role of media in our lives. Generally speaking, it is reasonable to suggest that media may not be the only factor in explaining certain kinds of behavior, such as violence or addiction to television viewing, but they may help *contribute* to these behaviors.

Important Concepts

I do not deal with every idea in each book I discuss – that would require an enormously long book. The books I deal with, and others from which I quote, are listed in the bibliography at the end of the book. You can consult them if you wish a more detailed look at their ideas.

I have written this book in a manner to make it accessible to the average reader; thus I have avoided, as much as possible, using the jargon that many academic scholars use in writing about media and culture. This jargon is often found in scholarly journals and is understood by the scholars who write articles in these journals and those who read the journals. But it is inappropriate to use this jargon very often in a book designed for undergraduate students and the general reader.

Learning About the Media is a Way of Learning About Ourselves

Since media are so much a part of our lives, learning about the media is indirectly a way or learning about ourselves – about where we got our ideas about what is important in life, about what we should expect out of life, and about how we should behave. Most people believe that their experiences play an important part in their lives; a chance remark can have incredible consequences (as the former leader of the Senate, Trent Lott, discovered). If that's the case, shouldn't mediated experiences count for something? That question is something you might keep in the back of your mind as you explore this fascinating and important subject – and learn how you can make sense of the media.

Ferdinand de Saussure . . . together with his two great contemporaries, Emile Durkheim in sociology and Sigmund Freud in psychology . . . helped to set the study of human behavior on a new footing. These three thinkers realized that one could not approach an adequate understanding of human practices and institutions if one treated human behavior as a series of events similar to events in the physical world . . . Human behavior is different. When studying human behavior the investigator cannot simply dismiss as subjective impressions the meaning it has for members of a society. If people see an action as impolite, that is a crucial fact, a social fact. To ignore the meanings actions and objects have in society would be to study mere physical events. Anyone analyzing human behavior is concerned not with events themselves but with events that have meaning.

Saussure, Freud, and Durkheim also saw that the study of human behavior misses its best opportunities if it tries to trace the historical causes of individual events. Instead, it must focus on the functions events have within a general social framework. It must treat social facts as part of a system of conventions and values . . .

How does one cope, systematically, with the apparent chaos of the modern world? This question was being asked in a variety of fields, and the replies which Saussure gives – that you cannot hope to attain an absolute or Godlike view of things but must choose a perspective, and that within this perspective objects are defined by their relations with one another, rather than by essences of some kind – are exemplary.

Jonathan Culler, Ferdinand de Saussure (1986: 15).

CHAPTER
1

Ferdinand de Saussure
Course in General Linguistics

I am starting this book with a person whom most people have never heard of, yet who is now generally recognized as one of the most important thinkers of the twentieth century – Ferdinand de Saussure. He was a linguistics professor who was born in Geneva, Switzerland, in 1857 and died in 1913, aged 56. He gave a series of lectures on linguistics between 1906 and 1911 that became his masterwork, *Course in General Linguistics*. This book is a collection of lecture notes from his students in those courses and some notes Saussure wrote before his untimely death. It was published in French in 1915 and in an English translation in 1959.

Saussure on Signs and Relations

Saussure introduced many ideas that have been of major importance: one is that we find meaning in life by seeing things as signs, which can be defined as anything that can be used to stand for something else. He called his theory of signs semiology – from the Greek term for signs, *semeîon*. An American philosopher, C. S. Peirce, who founded a different theory of signs, which he called semiotics, said "the universe is perfused [that is, permeated] with signs, if not composed exclusively of signs." So, for all practical purposes, everything is a sign and semiology attempts to figure out how signs work and how we interpret them. In recent years Peirce's term "semiotics" has become widely accepted as the term to use for analyzing and interpreting signs.

Another important idea that Saussure had was that *language is a system of signs in which the meaning of a term is based on its relations to other terms in the system.* Think, for example, of a sentence. Each word in the sentence affects every other word's meaning, and the order of words is often crucial. Consider the difference between "my husband was late" and "my late husband was." The words are the same but their order makes a great deal of difference. It is in the very nature of language, Saussure argued, that concepts take their meaning from their relationship to other terms, and the most important relationship for a term is a binary one – being a complementary opposite to another term. I will explain this in more detail shortly. But first, let's consider the science of semiology.

Semiology: The Science of Signs

What Saussure was interested in was how meaning was generated and communicated. He described his theory of semiology as follows (1966: 6):

> Language is a system of signs that express ideas, and is therefore comparable to a system of writing, the alphabet of deaf-mutes, military signals, etc. But it is the most important of all these systems.
>
> *A science that studies the life of signs within society* is conceivable . . . I shall call it *semiology* (from Greek, semeîon "sign"). Semiology would show what constitutes signs, what laws govern them.

Saussure suggested that signs are made up of two parts: a *signifier* (a sound, an object, an image) and a *signified* (a concept generated by the signifier). What is crucial, Saussure pointed out, is that the relationship between the signifier and the signified is arbitrary and based on convention. That means we have to learn what all signifiers mean, and signifiers can change their meaning over time. As Saussure explained (1966: 67):

> I call the combination of a concept and a sound-image a *sign*, but in current usage the term generally designates only a sound-image, a

word use for example (*arbor*, etc.). One tends to forget that *arbor* is called a sign only because it carried the concept "tree," with the result that the idea of sensory part implies the idea of the whole.

Ambiguity would disappear if the three notions here were designated by three names, each suggesting and opposing the others. I propose to retain the word sign (signe) to designate the whole and to replace *concept* and *sound-image* respectively by *signified* (*signifié*) and *signifier* (*signifiant*); the last two terms have the advantage of indicating the opposition that separates them from each other and from the whole of which they are parts.

From Saussure's perspective, human beings are sign-using, sign-generating, and sign-interpreting creatures – even though we may not be fully aware of the fact that we are doing so. And the world we live in is full of (or "perfused" with) signs each of which, though we may not think about it, has meaning for us.

For example, consider what we do when we are watching a television show or film. We look at the clothes the actors and actresses are wearing, at their body language, at their facial expressions, at their hair color, at how their hair is combed or styled, at any body ornaments they have, at how they speak and what they say, and so on. Each of these things is a sign and we use those signs to gain some kind of a sense of what the characters the actors are portraying are like. We do the same with people we see in the real world. And, in the real world, people are looking at us and doing the same thing. A person with purple hair and rings in her nose is conveying information about herself with these signs.

Saussure on Concepts

Saussure argued that language must be thought of as a self-contained system whose parts – or, for our purposes, concepts – gain meaning by being part of that system and through their relationship to that system. Nothing has meaning in itself or by itself. The system is all important since it gives words and concepts meaning. Our minds work in terms of relationships and the most important of these relationships is, as I mentioned earlier, being in opposition. As Saussure wrote (1996: 117):

> concepts are purely differential and defined not by their positive content but negatively by their relations with the other terms of the system. Their most precise characteristic is in being what the others are not.

This is a revolutionary statement that turned conventional linguistics, as it was practiced at the time, on its head, so to speak. Before Saussure, traditional linguists had taken an essentially historical perspective and traced how language use changed over time. Saussure said, and I'm simplifying things here, in addition to historical perspectives, we must look at how language works and how it shapes meaning. In effect, and this is something of a tongue-twister, concepts gain meaning by not being their opposite. It's kind of like the un-cola!

Language, Saussure explained, is a "system of interdependent terms in which the value of each term results solely from the simultaneous presence of the others" (1966: 114). This explains why it is that we always think in terms of opposites, such as rich and poor, happy and sad, beautiful and ugly, hero and villain. Consider this passage from Ecclesiastes here, which shows how our minds think in terms of oppositions:

To everything there is a season
And a time to every purpose under the heaven:
A time to be born, and a time to die;
A time to plant, and a time to pluck up that which is planted;
A time to kill, and a time to heal;
A time to break down, and a time to build up;
A time to weep, and a time to laugh;
A time to mourn, and a time to dance;
A time to cast away stones, and a time to gather stones together;
A time to embrace, and a time to refrain from embracing;
A time to seek, and a time to lose;
A time to keep, and a time to cast away;
A time to rend, and a time to sew;
A time to keep silence, and a time to speak;
A time to love, and a time to hate;
A time for war, and a time for peace.

We think in terms of conceptual oppositions because of the nature of language, which forces us to think that way. Another way to explain this is to think about how the words in a sentence affect the meaning of words. It is the system of words – that is, the sentence – that affects the meaning of words and concepts in that sentence. We now think of relationships of concepts and the system in which they are embedded to find meaning in things, and it is meaning on which Saussure focused his attention.

A comment made by Jonathan Culler in his book *Structuralist Poetics: Structuralism, Linguistics, and the Study of Literature* helps us understand the relation between language and mass-media works (1976: 4):

> The notion that linguistics might be useful in studying other cultural phenomena is based on two fundamental insights: first, that social and cultural phenomena are not simply material objects or events but objects and events with meaning, and hence signs; and second, that they do not have essences but are defined by a network of relations.

Armed with these insights about the nature of signs and how they convey meaning, we can analyze texts, and anything else – since semiotics is an all-inclusive, imperialistic, science.

King Andrew the First

IN PRACTICE

In this analysis I will take a political cartoon about Andrew Jackson by an unknown artist, done in 1832, and show how it generates meaning by using conventionally understood signs – or, technically speaking, signifiers. Artists use these signs as a shorthand way of conveying their ideas and making allusions to certain political events that would register with people who viewed this cartoon.

In this cartoon we find the following signifiers and signifieds:

Signifier	Signified
Crown, scepter, throne	Royalty
Ermine cape	Luxury
Right foot on Bank Bill	Trampling on democracy
Left foot on Constitution	Trampling on liberty
Veto scroll	Veto of Bank Bill
Robe	Feminization
King Andrew the First	Desire for absolute power

This cartoon suggests that President Andrew Jackson is an effete tyrant, an autocratic ruler who acted like a king. It reflects a certain political bias, like all political cartoons. In actuality Jackson was generally seen at the time as a defender of the common man and a person who attacked privilege and entrenched power.

In the work of Roland Barthes, myth is virtually synonymous with ideology and designates a level of symbolic or cultural connotation, active in a visual image or social narrative. Barthes developed this understanding of the term especially in the essays entitled Mythologies . . . *a study of the activities and events of contemporary French cultural life such as wrestling, striptease, a new Citroen motor car, films and advertising. This has proved an influential model for the study of popular culture. Though the term "myth" might not itself be used in this connection . . . the task of the cultural critic, following Barthes, is thought to be to "de-mythologize" the embedded meanings of activities and representations as they shape and structure daily life, showing how their implicit class and cultural attitudes have become "naturalized."*

Peter Brooker, Cultural Theory: A Glossary *(1999).*

CHAPTER 2

Roland Barthes
Mythologies

Roland Barthes is considered one of the most important critics of recent years. He produced a number of seminal works on semiotics, literature, criticism and cultural analysis that have influenced generations of scholars who came after him. *Mythologies* is probably his most famous work. In the preface to the 1970 edition of *Mythologies*, Barthes writes:

> This book has a double theoretical framework: on the one hand, an ideological critique bearing on the language of so-called mass culture; on the other, a first attempt to analyze semiologically the mechanics of this language. I had just read Saussure and as a result acquired the conviction that by treating "collective representations" as sign-systems, one might hope to go further than the pious show of unmasking them and account *in detail* for the mystification which transforms petit-bourgeois culture into a universal nature.

Barthes makes a number of points that are of interest to us here. First, he is making an ideological analysis of mass culture, by which he means an examination of its political bases and its role in the political process. Second, he is analyzing the mythic aspects of various aspects of popular culture and the mass media.

The Process of Mythologizing and Semiology

One thing the process of mythologizing does, he tells us in the book, is take phenomena that are cultural and historical and suggest they are natural. If something – an institution, for example – is historical or cultural, it means it was created by men and women and can be changed by them. If something is natural, on the other hand, it cannot be changed. There is a definite conservative bias to convincing people that things which are historical are really natural. The Marxist in Barthes would say that mythology produces "false consciousness," an unrealistic understanding of how the world works and one's role in society. This is useful to ruling classes, who wish to maintain the status quo and prevent the lower classes from organizing and perhaps revolting.

The second interesting point Barthes makes is that his analysis was influenced by having read Saussure and becoming convinced that "collective representations," by which he means films, television shows, objects, cultural practices, and the like, are sign-systems and therefore good subjects for semiological analysis. What semiology does is enable him to make detailed analyses of the process of mystification, of myth-making, that goes on, he argues, in bourgeois (capitalist) societies.

He wrote the essays that appeared in *Mythologies* at the rate of one per month over a two-year period – from 1954 to 1956, trying to "reflect regularly on some myths of French daily life" (1972: 11). Some of the topics he dealt with are wrestling, signs of Romans in films, ads for soap-powders and detergents, margarine, toys, steak and chips, striptease, and plastic. All of these topics, and the others in the book, played a role, Barthes argued, in mythologizing French culture and everyday life. Once you recognize that these things are signs and, more specifically signifiers, you can think about each of their signifieds. The second part of the book, "Myth Today," is theoretical and deals with topics such as "myth as a type of speech" and "myth as a semiological system."

Myth as a Semiological System

As Barthes explains (1972: 11):

> Myth is a language. So that while concerning myself with phenomena apparently most unlike literature (a wrestling-match, an elaborate dish, a plastics exhibition), I did not feel I was leaving the field of this general semiology of our bourgeois world.

What animates and informs Barthes' thinking in this book is ideological. He argues that our minds have become clouded by ideas, and most particularly myths, that the bourgeoisie – the ruling classes – want us to have. Their philosophy is hidden and so are they. As he writes (1972: 140):

> This anonymity of the bourgeoisie becomes even more marked when one passes from bourgeois culture proper to its derived, vulgarized and applied forms, to what one could call public philosophy, that which sustains everyday life, civil ceremonials, secular rites, in short the unwritten norms of interrelationships in a bourgeois society. It is an illusion to reduce the dominant culture to its inventive core: there also is a bourgeois culture, which consists of consumption alone. The whole of France is steeped in this anonymous ideology: our press, our films, our theatre, our pulp literature, our rituals, our Justice, our diplomacy, our conversations, our remarks about the weather, a murder trial, a touching wedding, the cooking we dream of, the garments we wear, everything, in everyday life, is dependent on the representation which the bourgeoisie *has and makes us have* of the relations between man and the world.

This bourgeois culture doesn't seem to be ideological, doesn't seem to have a political point of view; its secret is that is seems to be "that which goes without saying," or natural, as it "transforms the reality of the world into an image of the world, History into Nature" (1972: 141).

The World of Wrestling

Barthes' essay on wrestling is the first in the book, and the longest. It would seem remarkable that one of the most influential and important critics of recent years would write about something as seemingly trivial as professional wrestling – the kind we see on television. And yet, as Barthes shows, wrestling is an excellent subject for semiotic analysis. He starts his essay writing about how wrestling is a spectacle of excess, and is not really a sport but a theatrical production. He discusses the importance of the lighting and suggests that "light without shadow generates an emotion without reserve" (1972: 15). Wrestling is a performance of suffering similar to that we find in classical tragedies, he tells us.

Wrestling, he adds, involves excessive gestures and signs that function with absolute clarity. One important sign is the body of the wrestler, which indicates what kind of role he will play in the drama. "The physique of the wrestlers therefore constitutes a basic sign, which like a seed contains the whole fight," providing what the audience wants – an image of passion, not actual passion (1972: 18). He mentions a famous French wrestler, Thauvin:

> a fifty-year old with an obese and sagging body, whose type of asexual hideousness always inspires feminine nicknames, displays in his flesh the characters of baseness, for his part is to represent what, in the classical concept of the *salaud*, the "bastard" (the key-concept of any wrestling match), appears as organically repugnant. (1972: 17)

The French public calls Thauvin *la barbaque*, which means "stinking meat," and his body functions, then, as a sign of his baseness and his role in any match – cruelty and cowardice.

The "bastard" wrestler only accepts rules when they are useful to him and is unpredictable, and therefore, as Barthes explains, asocial. His inconsistency, Barthes says, is what drives audiences beside themselves with rage, for he has offended not its morality but its sense of logic, which it considers, Barthes suggests, the basest of crimes. What the French public looks for in wrestlers, he asserts, is a "highly moral image: that of the perfect 'bastard.' " Wrestling, then, because of the clarity of its signs and its many social, political, and cultural meanings, is a spectacle of considerable interest to the semiologist.

IN PRACTICE	A Semiotic Analysis of a Sea Shell

Whenever I taught a graduate seminar on media and semiotics, I played some semiotics games with my students. I wanted to show them that signs often are ambiguous and that people often interpret signs differently from the way we expect them to interpret them. I discussed some topics I mentioned earlier – the clothes we wear, the way we style our hair, the style of glasses we wear (if we wear glasses), the rings we place in our noses and our tongues, our tattoos, and other signs we use to send messages about ourselves. We always hope that other people will interpret correctly – that is, the way we want them to interpret them, but that is not always the case.

One game we played demonstrated that people often misinterpret signs. I asked my students to bring a simple object to class that they thought reflected something about themselves. I asked each student to bring the object in a plain brown-paper bag and to list, on a piece of paper in the bag, what the object signified.

One student brought a light gray seashell that was perhaps four inches long. I asked my students what they thought the shell signified. The answers my students gave were as follows: colorless, dead, empty, hollow, and brittle. The answers my student wrote on a piece of paper that she put in the paper bag were: natural, simple, elegant, and beautiful. She was quite astonished by the difference between what she thought the shell signified and the answer her classmates gave.

What my students learned from this exercise is that the relationship between signifiers (the shell) and signifieds (the concepts generated in their minds by the shell) are arbitrary, conventional, and open to considerable differences in opinion. C. S. Peirce wrote that a sign "is something which stands to somebody for something in some respect or capacity" (quoted in Zeman, 1977: 24). The sign interpreter plays an important role in making sense of signs and often doesn't interpret signs the way people who "send" or use signs think they will. This is a big problem when it comes to the mass media, where people often do not interpret signs correctly.

One other game I played with my students is relevant here. In one game I told them to pretend they were making a television show and they had to convey (only by using images and not using words) the idea of "Frenchness." I divided my class into groups of three and asked them

Continued

to do Frenchness and a number of other signifieds; I gave them the signified and asked them to provide signifiers that would generate that concept. Invariably, they had images of the little children with long baguettes, men in berets, and the Eiffel Tower.

The problem with these images were that they weren't necessarily limited to France. Men wear berets in Spain and other countries, so berets are not a good way to signify Frenchness. The Eiffel Tower is obviously in France, but does it signify Paris or France? They finally decided that the French flag signified France and that perhaps an image of a child with a long baguette, walking in a city where one can see the Eiffel Tower and shown in front of a building with a French flag would probably work. The gestalt – the collection of images, each reinforcing one another – did the job. The point of the game was to suggest that signifiers are slippery and don't always behave the way we think they will.

In Practice

But when my friend explains to me that life is like a pin-ball machine – that we are little balls shot out through an alley, kicked around from place to place, sometimes ringing a bell or flashing a light, and eventually falling into a trough and rolling out of sight – when he says this, I inquire whether his figure is not perhaps the perfect analogy. His figure has a lively meaning for us today because we believe in the laws of probability and half suspect the aimlessness of our existence.

Weller Embler, Metaphor and Meaning *(1966: 7).*

CHAPTER
3

George Lakoff and
Mark Johnson
Metaphors We Live By

The title of this book is well chosen, for the main argument the authors make is that metaphors, in interesting and often unrecognized ways, shape our thinking and our behavior. As they write (1980: 3):

> Metaphor is typically viewed as a characteristic of language alone, a matter of words rather than thought or action. For this reason, most people think they can get along perfectly well without metaphor. We have found, on the contrary, that metaphor is pervasive in everyday life, not just in language but in thought and action. Our ordinary conceptual system, in terms of which we both think and act, is fundamentally metaphoric in nature.
>
> The concepts that govern our thought are not just matters of the intellect. They also govern our everyday functioning, down to the most mundane details. Our concepts structure what we perceive, how we get around in the world, and how we relate to other people. Our conceptual system thus plays a central role in defining our

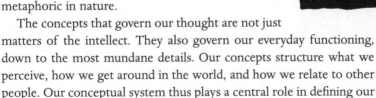

everyday realities. If we are right in suggesting that our conceptual system is largely metaphorical, what we experience and what we do every day is very much a matter of metaphor.

Their point, then, is that our behavior is shaped by concepts we have about how to live, and these concepts are essentially metaphorical. Metaphor is not just a poetical or rhetorical device.

Defining Metaphor and Metonymy

Metaphors are based on analogies – for example, the one that Weller Embler offered in the quotation that opened this chapter – life *is* a pinball game. The essence of analogy is seeing a relationship between two things, in seeing one thing in terms of something else. In metaphor this relationship is expressed directly and we say "life is a pinball game." There is a weaker form of metaphor called simile which uses "like" or "as" to deal with the relationship. It is a weaker analogy to say "Life *is like* a pinball game."

There is one other important way of thinking that pervades our thinking and that is metonymy. In metonymy the relationship between two things is based on association. As our authors explain (1980: 36):

Metaphor and metonymy are different *kinds* of processes. Metaphor is principally a way of conceiving of one thing in terms of another, and its primary function is understanding. Metonymy, on the other hand, has primarily a referential function, that is, it allows us to use one entity to *stand for* another. But metonymy is not merely a referential device. It also serves the function of providing understanding.

Just as a simile is a weaker form of a metaphor, there is a weaker form of metonymy called synecdoche (pronounced sin-eck-do-key), in which a part stands for the whole or the whole stands for a part. Let me offer some examples of metonymy and synecdoche.

Metonymy:	Rolls Royce (equals wealth).
Metonymy:	Snake in garden (suggests Garden of Eden).
Synecdoche:	She's just a pretty face (part for whole).

Metaphor and metonymy both shape our ideas, thoughts, concepts, and form a kind of lens through which we see the world. In the chart below I compare the two:

Metaphor	Metonymy
Analogy	Association
Life *is* a pinball game	Rolls Royce suggests wealth
Simile	Synecdoche
Uses like or as	Part for whole, whole for part
Life *is like* a pinball game	I've got a new set of wheels

What we have to recognize is that much of our thinking is based on metaphors and metonymies, even though we may not be conscious that this is so. They make life sensible to us and thus have a role to play in our thinking and our behavior. As Lakoff and Johnson write, "like metaphors, metonymic concepts structure not just our language but our thoughts, attitudes, and actions. And, like metaphoric concepts, metonymic concepts are grounded in our experience" (1980: 39).

They offer a number of examples of the way metaphors pervade our thinking. Let me cite some examples they give relative to love, which I've slightly modified in some cases:

1. *Love is a physical force.* I could feel the *electricity* between us.
2. *Love is a patient.* This is a *sick* relationship.
3. *Love is madness.* I'm *crazy* about her.
4. *Love is magic.* She *cast her spell* over me.
5. *Love is war.* He is known for his many rapid *conquests*.

You can see from these examples how metaphor pervades our language and our thinking and thus helps shape the way we see relationships and the world.

Metaphors Have Implications

Lakoff and Johnson make another important point – that metaphors have logical implications. As they explain (1980: 156):

Metaphors have entailments through which they highlight and make coherent certain aspects of our experience.

> A given metaphor may be the only way to highlight and coherently organize exactly those aspects of our experience.
>
> Metaphors may create realities for us, especially social realities. A metaphor may thus be a guide for future action. Such actions will, of course, fit the metaphor. This will, in turn, reinforce the power of the metaphor to make experience coherent. In this sense metaphors can be self-fulfilling prophecies.

This is an important insight. Metaphors not only shape the way we see things but also have logical implications and thus function as guides to future actions on our part, even though we may not be aware that this is happening. It may very well be that one of the problems people face is that they have, one way or another, picked up certain self-destructive metaphors that they apply to themselves.

Metaphor, Metonymy, and Media

If our conversation and thinking are, to a great degree, metaphorical and metonymic, it is only natural to expect that we will find these thought processes pervading the mass media. In fact, it can be argued that the mass media provide us with many of the metaphors that we adopt in thinking about life and trying to make sense of experience. These metaphors are found in the dialogue between characters in mass-mediated texts, but also can be conveyed by images.

For example, there is a fascinating print advertisement for Fidji perfume that shows a Polynesian woman, holding a bottle of perfume, with a snake around her neck. That snake has two functions of interest to us here. It is, metaphorically, a phallic symbol. (Snakes are conventionally understood to be phallic symbols.) And it is also, metonymically speaking, a suggestion of the Garden of Eden, where, as we all know, Eve was tempted by a snake. So an object can have both metaphoric and metonymic functions. We can see that metaphor and metonymy enable authors and artists to convey a great deal of information by taking advantage of the knowledge people have and their ability to interpret metaphors and metonymies correctly – though with the mass media, there is always a great deal of misinterpretation that goes on.

If you make a commercial and show someone driving a Rolls Royce, generally speaking, people know what you are conveying – that this person is probably very wealthy. By showing – that is, using metonymy – you don't have to spell it out. Print advertisements and television commercials make considerable use of these processes since they are economical ways of conveying ideas and attitudes.

Love is a Game

I am going to spell out, in some detail, the logical implications of the metaphor "Love is a game." There was a song that was very popular a number of years ago – "All in the Game" – which said, quite directly, that love is a game. If you accept the notion that love is a game, what does it suggest about love?

1. *Someone wins and someone loses.*
In most games, there is an element of competition and at the end of the game, someone wins and the other players lose. What does it mean to "lose" at the game of love? And what does it mean to "win" at love?

2. *Games have rules.*
Games have rules that you must follow to play them correctly. These rules are generally spelled out in books of games whose rules become accepted. Without rules, games don't have any structure and can't be played.

3. *Sometimes players cheat.*
This is a common theme in songs – about people who cheat in the "game" of love. Songs about "cheating hearts" indirectly suggest that love is a game.

4. *Games come to an end after a period of playing.*
Games don't last forever, and end after someone "wins" and other "loses." If love is a game, and games always end, the implication is that love doesn't last very long.

5. *People aren't serious when they play games.*
Games are entertainments and are meant to amuse and entertain people while they are being played. They are not part of "real life" but are momentary diversions.

Continued

Lakoff and Johnson

6. *Games often involve trickery and deceit.*

One important element of many games involves the matter of deception and trickery. In poker, for example, deception is a major factor in the game and players who win may not always hold the best cards.

7. *Games often involve boards or places where the game is played.*

Games like *Monopoly* and *Chutes and Ladders* are played on boards. The "game" of love is also generally "played" in certain places and not in others.

We can see, then, that the metaphor "love is a game" implies that certain things connected to games will follow; some of these logical implications are not very positive and may be quite destructive. This metaphor about love is in conflict with other metaphors about love that suggest it is endless and lasts "until the end of time."

From morning to night, narrations constantly haunt streets and buildings. They articulate our existences by teaching us what they must be. They "cover the event," that is to say, they make our legends *(*legenda, *what is to be read and said) out of it. Captured by the radio (the voice is the law) as soon as he awakens, the listener walks all day long through the forest of narrativities from journalism, advertising, and television narrativities that still find time, as he is getting ready for bed, to slip a few final messages under the portals of sleep. Even more than the God told about by the theologians of earlier days, these stories have a providential and predestining function: they organize in advance our work, our celebrations, and even our dreams. Social life multiplies the gestures and modes of behavior (im)printed by narrative models; it ceaselessly reproduces and accumulates "copies" of stories. Our society has become a recited society, in three senses: it is defined by* stories *(*récits, *the fables constituted by our advertising and informational media), by* citations *of stories, and by the interminable* recitation *of stories.*

Michel de Certeau, The Practice of Everyday Life *(1984: 186).*

CHAPTER 4

Aristotle
Poetics

In the quotation facing this page, Michel de Certeau makes an important point – that our lives are pervaded by narratives, found in radio and television commercials, television shows, films, novels, and other texts. And these narratives play an important role in shaping our psyches and our social lives. They "imprint" themselves on us, so narratives are very important and deserve a good deal of attention. We may consider Aristotle to be the first important analyst of narratives and thus, by implication, the prototype of the modern media critic. (Some might bestow this honor on Plato, Aristotle's teacher, I might add.) Aristotle focused his attention on the dominant kinds of narrative texts

carried by the media in his day – poetry and theater – but his insights can be applied to all the texts (most of which turn out to be narratives) carried by the media in contemporary times. Our media are dominated by narratives – that is, by stories. But what is a story, what kinds of stories are there, and why are these stories important? This is where Aristotle's *Poetics*, his treatise on narrative criticism (published between 335 and 332 BC), become interesting to us. I will quote Aristotle in some detail since the language he uses is a very important part of his argument.

Aristotle starts *Poetics* with a discussion of his notion that works of art are imitations of reality. He writes (1951: 28–9):

> Epic poetry and Tragedy, Comedy also and Dithyrambic poetry and the music of the flute and of the lyre in most of their forms are all in their general conception modes of imitation. They differ, however, from one another in three respects – the medium, the objects, the manner or mode of imitation, being in each case distinct.

This notion, that our arts are "imitations" of reality, is known as the "mimetic" theory of art, because *mimesis* is the Greek term for imitation. Aristotle suggests that this "instinct" of imitation is implanted in our childhood and distinguishes humans from animals. Other theorists of media and the arts have disputed this notion and argued that the arts are not imitations of reality, not mirrors, but lamps – projections of the realities of artists.

Aristotle then discusses what works of art imitate – namely "men in action." He writes (1951: 30):

> Since the objects of imitation are men in action, and these men must be either of a higher or a lower type (for moral character mainly answers to these divisions, goodness and badness being the distinguishing marks of moral differences), it follows that we must represent men as either better than in real life, or as worse, or as they are.

Aristotle then suggests that the difference between comedy and tragedy is that comedy represents men as worse than in real life, men who are made ridiculous, and tragedy represents men as better than in actual life.

Next, Aristotle makes a distinction that has implications for modern notions of the difference between popular culture (also known as mass-mediated culture) and the elite arts. When Aristotle uses the term "poetry" we can understand it to mean the creative arts in general, including television programs, films, songs, and plays – all of which tend to have a narrative thrust to them. He explains (1951: 31–2):

> Poetry now diverged in two directions, according to the individual character of the writers. The graver spirits imitated noble actions, and the actions of good men. The more trivial sort imitated the actions of meaner person, at first composing satires, as the former did hymns to

the gods and the praises of famous men . . . Comedy is, as we have said, an imitation of characters of a lower type – not however in the full sense of the word bad, the ludicrous being merely a subdivision of the ugly. It consists of some defect or ugliness which is not painful or destructive. To take an obvious example, the comic mask is ugly and distorted, but does not imply pain.

This suggestion that there were important differences between serious art and trivial art can be seen as one of the first statements that differentiated popular culture and the popular arts from elite culture and elite arts, such as poetry, opera, serious novels, and theater. Aristotle is reputed to have written a book on Comedy, since he mentions having done so, but this book has been lost.

What interests Aristotle most in *Poetics* is tragedy, and tragedy, he asserts, has certain characteristics (1951: 34):

Tragedy then is an imitation of an action that is serious, complete, and of a certain magnitude; in language embellished with each kind of artistic ornament, the several kinds being found in separate parts of the play; in the form of action, not of narrative; through pity and fear effecting the proper purgation of these emotions.

This notion that a tragedy leads to a purgation of emotions is the basis, I might point out, of the argument made by many contemporary media scholars that violence on television does not have harmful effects since it leads to a catharsis – a purgation of emotions. Those who attack violence on television also use Aristotle's notions, suggesting that people often "imitate" actions they see on television.

Aristotle now deals with the implications of tragic imitation. It implies persons acting and requires, he adds, "Spectacular equipment," which we can translate to mean all the special effects, music, lighting, computer animation, and other techniques used in making films and television programs. As he explains (1951: 34):

Again, tragedy is the imitation of an action; and an action implies personal agents, who necessarily possess certain distinctive qualities both of character and thought; for it is by these that we qualify actions themselves, and these – thought and character – are the two natural causes from which actions spring, and on actions again all success or failure

---

depends. Hence the Plot is the imitation of the action: – for by plot I here mean the arrangement of the incidents. By Character I mean that in virtue of which we ascribe certain qualities to the agents . . . Every Tragedy, therefore, must have six parts, which parts determine its quality – namely, Plot, Character, Diction, Thought, Spectacle, Song.

Aristotle is most insistent that the most important aspect of tragedy, and by implication we can say all stories, is the plot – namely the arrangement of incidents in a narrative. But the diction, that is, the language used by the characters, their personalities (and tragedies involve the fall of a person of some consequence), the ideas expressed in the story, and the use of spectacle and song (which we can interpret to mean music) also are not only important but required.

This notion that tragedies *must* have the six components listed by Aristotle in the selections quoted above not only affected playwrights but also had profound implications on the thought of literary critics – the precursors of media critics – for hundreds of years. Aristotle's notion that "character is subsidiary to the actions" in a story also has been the subject of considerable controversy, and there are now two opposing schools of thought about the matter, whose ideas are found in numerous books on writing for television and film. One school argues that the plot creates the characters in a text and the other school argues that stories must be character-driven and that it is characters whose actions – based on their temperaments – create plots.

There were other aspects of tragedy that Aristotle dealt with. One involves completeness – the action that tragedy imitates must be complete and whole, and thus have a beginning, a middle, and an end. Another is that plots can be simple – continuous and without a reversal or fortune or a recognition scene – or complex, in which there are changes accompanied by a reversal, a recognition scene, or both.

The worst kind of texts, Aristotle suggested, were episodic ones in which there is no necessary sequence to the actions and there is little concern with probability or necessity. The situation comedies and many dramatic action series found on television would be good examples of episodic texts. These texts are resolved all too often, he suggests, by using a *deus ex machina* – literally a "god out of a machine" by which he meant an artificial device. In the great tragedies, the ending is satisfactory because it arises from elements in the plot, with some kind of a reversal and a recognition on the part of the hero; it is not something just tacked on artificially to bring a story to a conclusion.

In his *Poetics*, Aristotle offered a number of distinctions involving comedies and tragedies and rules for the construction of narratives that played, and to some extent still continue to play, an important part in our thinking about theater, and by extension narratives of all kinds in all media. *Poetics* is a seminal work that has had enormous influence for several thousand years. Most people, when they criticize a film or analyze a television program are, without realizing what they are doing, dealing with one of more of the topics or issues Aristotle brought to our attention in *Poetics*.

Theories about Comedy: Why Do We Laugh?

Aristotle's book, *Comedy*, has been lost, so most of what we know about his ideas on the matter are found in his *Poetics*. The quotation from Certeau at the start of this chapter points out that narratives haunt us, day and night. What he doesn't mention is that many of these narratives are humorous in nature. In our newspapers we generally find one or two pages devoted to comic strips, most of which are humorous. There are also humorous cartoons and political cartoons, many of which are satirical and have a comic nature.

Why Do We Laugh?

For our purposes, let's assume that the term "comic" refers to texts that are humorous and humor involves everything – texts (situation comedies, film comedies, comic novels, witty statements people make, etc.) that makes us laugh. A question immediately suggests itself: Why do we laugh? Aristotle has given us an answer to this question. We laugh, he argues, because we feel superior to others, those who have been made ridiculous. Comedy, he reminds us, is "an imitation of men worse than average."

Other philosophers and speculators have come up with different explanations for why we laugh. Perhaps the most widely accepted theory involves incongruity – a difference between what we expect and what we get. We see this in jokes, which generally end in punch lines that surprise us and, if the jokes are good, make us laugh. Schopenhauer explained the theory very directly. He wrote:

Continued

> The cause of laughter in every case is simply the sudden perception of the incongruity between a concept and the real objects which have been thought through it in some relation, and laughter is just the expression of this incongruity. (Piddington 1933: 171–2)

Other philosophers have made similar arguments.

A third notion that explains why we laugh comes from psychoanalytic theory and the work of Freud and others. Freud wrote a book, *Jokes and Their Relation to the Unconscious*, in which he suggested that humor involves masked aggression. As he explained (1963: 101):

> And here at last we can understand what it is that jokes achieve in the service of their purpose. They make possible the satisfaction of an instinct (whether lustful or hostile) in the face of an obstacle that stands in its way.

If you think about the monologues of television comedians, you find a great deal of masked aggression – and sometimes aggression that isn't masked that much. But if the aggression is too obvious, too overt, the notion that we are dealing with something humorous disappears, so comedians have to mask their aggression in clever ways. Freud's book has a great many wonderful Jewish jokes in it. He points out in this book (1963: 112), "I do not know whether there are many other instances of a people making fun to such a degree of its own character." The Jewish sense of humor has been linked by some scholars to the very survival of the Jewish people in the face of continual adversity over thousands of years.

A fourth theory that explains why we laugh involves work by communication theorists, neuroscientists, and people such as anthropologist Gregory Bateson and psychiatrist William Fry. It deals with how human beings process information. This theory considers how communication, paradox, play, and the resolution of logical problems are involved with humor.

Laughter and Liberation

Although we haven't solved the problem of why people laugh, one thing is certain. People crave humor and laughter, which explains why there are so many situation comedies on television and why film comedies have such widespread appeal. The Russian literary critic Mikhail Bakhtin offered another important insight into humor. Laughter, he says, liberates . . . and it enables us to find truths that are not accessible by any other means. He contrasts laughter with medieval (and one could add modern) seriousness in *Rabelais and His World* (1984: 94–5):

> As opposed to laughter, medieval seriousness was infused with elements of fear, weakness, humility, submission, falsehood, hypocrisy, or on the other hand with violence, intimidation, threats, prohibitions. As a spokesman of power, seriousness terrorized, demanded and forbade . . . Distrust of the serious tone and confidence in the truth of laughter had a spontaneous, elemental character. It was understood that fear never lurks behind laughter . . . and that hypocrisy and lies never laugh but wear a serious mask. Laughter created no dogmas and could not become authoritarian; it did not convey fear but a feeling of strength. It was linked with the procreating act, with birth, renewal, fertility, abundance. Laughter was also related to food and drink and the people's earthy immortality, and finally it was related to the future of things to come and was to clear the way for them.

It is laughter that is behind Bakhtin's theory of carnivalization, his notion that our desire for celebration, for food and for drink and play, is central in our lives. This desire is found not only during carnival periods but, in modified forms, at all times; this desire for pleasure is also, he tells us, at the center of all the popular arts and all popular forms of entertainment and amusement.

On the most obvious level television is a dramatic medium simply because a large proportion of the material it transmits is in the form of traditional drama mimetically represented by actors and employing plot, dialogue, character, gesture, costume – the whole panoply of dramatic means of expression . . . According to the 1980 edition of The Media Book, in the Spring of 1989 American men on average watched television for over 21 hours per week, while the average American woman's viewing time reached just over 25 hours per week. The time devoted by the average American adult male to watching dramatic material on television thus amounts to over 12 hours per week, while the average American woman sees almost 16 hours of drama on television each week. That means the average American adult sees the equivalent of five to six full-length stage plays a week!

Martin Esslin, The Age of Television (1982: 7).

CHAPTER 5

Tzvetan Todorov
Introduction to Poetics

Up to this point, we have focused a good deal of attention on language and its role in shaping our attempts to find meaning in things – and, in particular, mass-mediated texts. Saussure helped us understand that mass-mediated texts are full of signs; Barthes explained to us that these texts often have a mythological significance, whose purpose is to hide their ideological content; and Lakoff and Johnson showed us how metaphors and metonymies shape our thinking. We find many of these metaphors in our songs, commercials, television shows, and films that are part of our everyday lives. Todorov, in his book *Introduction to Poetics* (1981), helps us understand exactly what literary criticism, and by implication media criticism, attempts to do.

Different Kinds of Media Analysis

There are many different aspects to media analysis. We can focus our attention on the texts the media carry, we can look at the impact of the media on audiences, we can consider the nature of the media themselves, we can examine the role of artists and other creative workers in fashioning mass-mediated texts, and we can examine social, economic, and political aspects of the media. In recent years there has been an incredible consolidation in the ownership of the media. What effects have this consolidation had?

I would suggest that all of these different focal points are related to one another. We will move on to some of these topics after we have examined, in more detail, ways of making sense of the texts that are found in the media. As the Esslin quotation at the beginning of this chapter points out, when we watch television we watch narratives, for the most part. The same applies, of course, to films, and also to songs and video games. They are all narratives that can be classified into certain categories that we call genres.. So understanding how to analyze narratives is of some importance.

Poetics

Poetics, for our purposes, is just a fancy term for analysis, and, in particular, for interpretation, for understanding how texts work their magic. As Todorov explains, there are other terms for interpretation, such as *"exegesis, commentary, explication de texte, close reading, analysis,* or even just *criticism"* (1981: 3) He points out that there are various forms of criticism, such as psychological or psychoanalytic, sociological or ethnological, and philosophical, to which we can add Marxist, feminist, and semiotic. These methods of analysis, he suggests, don't focus on the text itself but, instead, use texts to deal with concepts in their particular discipline. As he writes (1981: 6):

> All deny the autonomous character of the literary work and regard it as the manifestation of laws that are external to it and that concern the psyche, or society, or even "the human mind." The object of such studies is to transpose the work into the realm considered fundamental: it is a labor of decipherment and translation; the literary work is the expression of "something," and the goal of such studies is to reach this "something" through the poetic code. Depending on whether the nature of this object to be reached is philosophical, psychological, sociological, or something else, the study in question will be inscribed within one of these types of discourse.

According to Todorov, then, people from various disciplines use mass-mediated texts for their own purposes, and aren't interested in these texts in themselves – aren't interested in how they work and how they create their effects, the way people involved with poetics do.

An Obsession with Theory and the Matter of Exegesis

Our interest in poetics and in literature – and I include pop culture and mass-mediated texts in this general definition of literature – has been waning. (Popular culture texts used to be called sub-literature years ago.) One could argue, with some justification, that in recent years literary and media scholars have become more interested in theoretical matters related to texts than in the works themselves. Todorov discusses exegesis, or interpretation and criticism, and its relation to theory (1981: xxii):

> Exegesis always presupposes a theory (however unconscious), for it needs descriptive concepts, or more simply a vocabulary, in order to refer to the work studied; now definitions of concepts are precisely what constitute theory. But theory also presupposes the existence of exegesis . . . Each of the two can correct the other: the theoretician criticizes the exegete's discourse, and the exegete in his turn shows the inadequacies of theory in relation to the object studied, the works.

What this passage suggests is that critics of the media who focus on theory tend to neglect texts, and textual critics, who focus their attention on analyzing a given work, tend to neglect theory. They both need one another.

The fact is, all criticism is based on some theory, some notion or notions that are held to be fundamental; criticism doesn't just appear out of the blue. Critics always have some point of view – whether it is a discipline or a philosophical belief – that shapes their criticism. I am not talking about things like film reviews in newspapers and magazines here, though film reviewers also have certain notions that shape their reviews – namely that the dialogue should be stimulating, that the story should be interesting, that the acting should be good, and so on. The question is – what makes dialogue stimulating (or whatever word you wish to use to describe "good" dialogue) and what makes a story interesting? These questions are the kind of questions dealt with by literary – for our purposes media – and rhetorical criticism.

The Reader's Role

Todorov points out that when we interpret a text we always are affected by the culture or subculture in which we live, and the values and beliefs that are dominant. As he writes (1981: xxx):

> Every work is rewritten by its reader, who imposes upon it a new grid of interpretation for which he is not generally responsible but which comes to him from his culture, from his time, in short from another discourse; all comprehension is the encounter of two discourses: a dialogue . . . interpretation is no longer true or false but rich or poor, revealing or sterile, stimulating or dull.

This explains why analyzing media texts is so difficult; in a sense, there are no wrong answers, but some criticisms or interpretations are better, more interesting, more suggestive, than others. It is the degree to which an interpretation covers all the important events that happen in a text (including technical matters like editing, sound, and music) and makes sense of them that counts.

The Problem of Taste

There's no accounting for taste . . . by which we mean everyone has the right to his or her own opinion and we can't always explain why people have the taste they do. But, as Todorov points out, some opinions are better than others. As we get older and as we become more educated and more sophisticated, our tastes generally change and evolve. When we are children we like certain foods, but when we are older, with more experiences, our tastes usually change and many of us come to prefer filet mignon or sushi to hot dogs and hamburgers.

I had an interesting conversation involving literary taste. I was at a gathering and someone asked me "What do you think of Shakespeare?" I replied "Most literary scholars would say he's the greatest playwright who ever lived . . . and I agree with them." He shook his head. "I think his stuff is lousy. I think Steve Martin is a much better playwright than Shakespeare." I laughed and thought to myself, "there's no point in arguing with him." So I ended the conversation.

We have learned, from Todorov, some important lessons about criticism: namely that criticism isn't right or wrong but rich and revealing or poor and sterile; that critics always operate from some theoretical position that shapes their criticism; and that for some critics, texts are of interest mainly because they enable them to talk about some social, political, economic, or theoretical issue dear to their hearts.

What Happens in Hamlet

Todorov has suggested we look at texts in terms of how they work and generate meaning, so I will examine *Hamlet* in that manner, rather than interpreting it from a psychoanalytic, Marxist, feminist, or some other perspective. (I do this in a comic mystery I wrote, *The Hamlet Case*.) Saussure said "in language there are only differences," and the same applies to characters and events in a text. Without oppositions, without differences, nothing means anything and nobody in the text stands for anything In the table that follows I suggest the basic oppositions found in *Hamlet* that help audiences find meaning in this enigmatic work.

Hamlet	
Ghost of the father	Live uncle: Claudius
Revelation (uncover)	Deception (cover up)
Victim	Murderer
Action by Hamlet	Inaction by Hamlet
Gravedigger	Polonius
Earthly wisdom	Official wisdom
Revenge and justice	Ambition and lust
Players in play within play	Actual king and queen
Ophelia	Gertrude
Sexual love	Oedipal love
Horatio	Rosencrantz and Guildenstern
Fortinbras	

Interpreting the Oppositions

I start with the opposition between Hamlet's father, the ghost who cries out for revenge, and his uncle Claudius, who has murdered Hamlet's father and married Hamlet's mother, Gertrude. Hamlet's father, the

Continued

---

ghost, stands for revelation and Claudius stands for deception. Hamlet's father is the victim, his uncle is the murderer. The central problem in the play is between Hamlet's vow to uncover what has happened (to expose Claudius) and then "take action," and his inability to do so.

The Gravedigger stands for earthly wisdom while Polonius stands for "official" and pedantic wisdom. Polonius is always spouting off maxims for good behavior that sound good but are difficult, if not impossible, to implement. Hamlet's actions are motivated by revenge and justice while Claudius' actions are motivated by ambition and sexual lust. Hamlet instructs the players to put on a drama involving a fictional king and queen who murder someone and are modeled after two real ones – Claudius and Gertrude. Hamlet says his play will "catch the conscience of the king," and so it does. Ophelia represents sexual love, and Gertrude, at least as far as Hamlet is concerned, represents what some have construed as an incestuous Oedipal attachment he has. Horatio is on the side where we find Hamlet, while Rosencrantz and Guildenstern are shown as opposing him. Finally, in the middle of the two sets of polar oppositions we find Fortinbras, back from Poland, who has, as Hamlet puts it "my dying voice." It is Hamlet who is the center of attention when the play starts and it is Fortinbras who has this role as the play ends.

An Opposition of Some Importance

The question we must ask now is whether the structure I have elicited from the play is *in the play or in my mind*. That is a problem all analyses of texts have to face. We don't ask this about Shakespeare, for creative artists don't always understand the true significance of the works they create. They work, in many cases, using subconscious or unconscious elements of their psyches. But critics have to answer this question: Are analyses of texts, such as the one offered above, found in the texts themselves or in the minds of those who make the analyses. The way critics deal with this matter, I would suggest, is by offering evidence – from the text – to support their analysis. Let me offer the metaphor of a trial: In the case of conflicting analyses of a text, whoever makes the most convincing argument "wins."

Culture patterns normally manifest themselves in a variety of cultural materials. Propp's analysis should be useful in analyzing the structure of literary forms (such as novels and plays), comic strips, motion-picture and television plots, and the like. In understanding the interrelationship between folklore and literature, and between folklore and the mass media, the emphasis has hitherto been principally on content. Propp's Morphology suggests that there can be structural borrowings as well as content borrowings.

Alan Dundes, "Introduction to the Second Edition,"
Vladimir Propp, Morphology of the Folktale *(1968: xiv–xv)*.

CHAPTER
6

Vladimir Propp
Morphology of the Folktale

The media, I have pointed out, carry texts – works of art of one kind or another, generally narratives. What Propp, a Russian folklorist, did was figure out a way to understand how narratives are organized. He did this by taking a group of Russian folktales and analyzing their morphology, that is, their form and structure. He worked with folktales but his methodology can be applied to other kinds of narrative – in particular, the narratives we find in films and television programs, comic books, novels, and the like, as Alan Dundes has suggested in the quotation that begins this chapter. Propp's *Morphology of the Folktale* was published in Russian in 1928 and in an English translation in 1968.

The term "morphology" means structure. Propp tried classifying the folktales he was studying according to their themes but found there were many overlapping themes and that didn't work. He tried a classification system that put the tales into various categories but he couldn't do so; he tried various other things to make sense of these tales, also without success. Finally, he arrived at a methodology that worked – looking at their structural components. As he explained (1968: 21), "Tales possess one special characteristic: components of one tale can without any alteration whatsoever, be transferred to another."

Language and Morphology

Saussure and other linguists pointed out that language is a system in which the interrelationship of the component parts establish meaning. We have to learn languages, which means we have to learn what words mean and how they fit together. This description of language is similar in nature to what Propp did. He analyzed the component parts of his fairy tales (1968: 19):

> For the sake of comparison we shall separate the component parts of fairy tales by special methods; and then, we shall make a comparison of tales according to their components. The result will be a morphology (i.e. a description of the tale according to its component parts and the relationship of these components to each other and the whole).

So it is how components of tales fit together that is what is important.

The most important thing, Propp suggested, was the functions of the different characters in a tale. Different characters may perform these functions in different tales, but the crucial matter is that one way or another the functions are performed. As Propp wrote (1968: 21):

> the functions of the dramatis personae are basic components of the tale, and we must first of all extract them. In order to extract them we must define them. Definition must proceed from two points of view. First of all, definition should in no case depend on the personage who carries out the function. Definition of a function will most often be given in the form of a noun expressing an action (interdiction, interrogation, flight, etc.). Secondly, an action cannot be defined apart from its place in the course of narration.

Thus, a function is an act of a character understood in terms of its significance for the course of action in a narrative text.

These functions, Propp adds (1968: 21), have two characteristics:

> Functions of characters serve as stable, constant elements in a tale, and are independent of how they and by whom they are fulfilled. They constitute the fundamental components of a tale. The number of function known to the fairy tale is limited.

Propp argues here that all tales are composed of certain functions (that is, acts of characters) and the number of functions is limited. In essence, what

Propp is suggesting is that there are certain building blocks that are used to make a tale, and these building blocks are limited in number.

He adds, later, that the sequence of these functions is always the same, and that all fairy tales are of a similar structure. We need not consider these last two notions in using Propp's functions, and we must also understand that some of the functions Propp describes have to be modernized and updated to be useful in analyzing modern narratives. If we extrapolate from Propp's book, we must conclude that all narratives have certain common components in them and the number of these components is limited.

Propp's Functions

In essence, Propp made a content analyses of the actions of the characters in his collection of fairy tales and came up with what he called "an initial situation," that starts the tale off (and isn't a function), and 31 functions of characters. Different characters in different stories perform the same function; that is, a function is not tied to only one character.

In the list that follows, I offer a simplified version of Propp's initial situation and 31 functions. He gives detailed descriptions of each function in his book, but we can figure out, fairly easily, what actions a function describes.

Initial Situation:	Members of family introduced, the hero introduced.
1. Absentation:	One of the members of the family absentsself.
2. Interdiction:	Interdiction is addressed to hero. (Can be reversed.)
3. Violation:	The interdiction is violated.
4. Reconnaissance:	Villain makes attempt to get information
5. Delivery:	Villain obtains information about his victim.
6. Trickery:	Villain tries to deceive his victim.
7. Complicity:	Victim is deceived.
8. Villainy:	Villain causes harm to a member of a family.
Lack:	A member of family lacks or desires something.
9. Mediation:	A misfortune made known. The hero is dispatched.
10. Counteraction:	Hero (Seeker) agrees to counteraction.
11. Departure:	Hero (Seeker) leaves home.

---

12. 1st donor function:	Hero tested, then receives magical agent or gets helper.
13. Hero's reaction:	Hero reacts to agent or donor.
14. Receipt of agent:	Hero acquires use of magical agent.
15. Spatial change:	Hero is led to object of search.
16. Struggle:	Hero and villain join in direct combat.
17. Branding:	Hero is branded.
18. Victory:	Villain is defeated.
19. Liquidation:	Initial misfortune or lack is liquidated.
20. Return:	Hero returns.
21. Pursuit, chase:	Hero is pursued.
22. Rescue:	Hero rescued from pursuit.
23. Unrecognized arrival:	Hero, unrecognized, arrives home or elsewhere.
24. Unfounded claims:	False hero presents unfounded claims.
25. Difficult task:	Difficult task is proposed to hero.
26. Solution:	The task is resolved.
27. Recognition:	Hero is recognized.
28. Exposure:	False hero or villain is exposed.
29. Transfiguration:	Hero is given a new appearance.
30. Punishment:	Villain is punished.
31. Wedding:	Hero is married, ascends the throne.

Propp said that there were two kinds of heroes and all tales had either a victimized hero, who suffers from the hand of a villain, or a seeker hero, who leaves home in pursuit of some quest, but never both. The victimized hero may also travel but his travels aren't the same as travels of the seeker hero. As Propp writes (1968: 50):

> The hero of a fairy tale is that character who either directly suffers from the action of the villain in the complication (the one who senses some kind of lack), or who agrees to liquidate the misfortune or lack of another person. In the course of the action the hero is the person who is supplied with a magical agent (a magical helper), and who makes use of it or is served by it.

Think, for example, of the various *Star Wars* films in which Luke Skywalker obtains both a magical agent (his light saber) and all kinds of magical helpers in the different films to help him battle the villain, Darth Vader, and his various evil henchmen.

Propp devotes the remainder of his book to various complications related to his functions, but they are not of importance for us. What is significant is that we can find in narratives of all kinds many of Propp's functions – including variations and modifications of them – and that the fairy tale may very well serve as the model upon which all other kinds of narratives are built. If this is correct, we learn that many of the stories we read in novels and see in films and television shows come from fairy tales or have strong fairy-tale elements in them. To demonstrate this, we can use Propp's functions to find these elements in most of the stories to which we are exposed.

Recognizing that our stories are, more often than not, updated fairy tales is important because of the roles that fairy tales play in our lives. As Bruno Bettelheim, a distinguished psychologist, once explained, they deal with universal problems and carry messages to unconscious elements in our psyches and give us courage to face the difficulties that life poses for all of us. When we are young we learn from fairy tales that despite the problems people face, eventually good will triumph over evil and everyone will live happily ever after. Thanks to Propp, we can understand that the texts carried in the mass media – though we may not recognize that such is the case – often have therapeutic value because they are modified and updated fairy tales.

Understanding Genres

IN PRACTICE

Fairy tales, we must remember, are a *kind* of story – or in the language of media criticism, a *genre*. This French word means "kind" or "type." In our everyday lives, we often make our decisions about what kinds of television shows to watch, films to see, or video games to play, based on how we may feel or certain attractions a genre holds for us. For complicated reasons, people develop a fondness for certain kinds of stories. When we are children, fairy tales are very important for us, and have great therapeutic value. When we are older, we move on to more complicated kinds of stories, with different kinds of characters that provide different kinds of gratification.

Continued

In the table that follows I offer suggestions about the formulaic aspects of some important genres: the kinds of characters we find in them, their plots and their themes, and so on. Thinking about stories in terms of their genres, and what happens in certain genres, helps us understand something about their appeal, as the Radway study of romance novel-readers that follows this chapter shows.

Genre	Romance	Western	Science Fiction	Spy
Time	Early 1900s	1800s	Future	Present
Location	Rural England	Edge of civilization	Outer space	World
Hero	Lords, upper-class types	Cowboy	Space man	Agent
Heroine	Damsel in distress	Schoolmarm	Space gal	Woman spy
Secondary	Friends of heroine	Town people, Indians	Technicians	Assistant agents
Villains	Lying, seeming friend	Outlaws	Aliens	Moles
Plot	Heroine finds love	Restore law and order	Repel aliens	Find moles
Theme	Love conquers all	Justice and progress	Save humanity	Save free world
Costume	Gorgeous dresses	Cowboy hat	Space gear	Trench coat
Locomotion	Cars, horses, carriages	Horse	Rocket ship	Sports car
Weaponry	Fists	Six-gun	Ray gun, laser gun	Pistol with silencer

This table shows some of the basic conventions found in formulaic genres. These conventions establish what a genre means for people and enable them to understand the texts without too much expenditure of intellectual effort. Thus, a person who goes to see a science-fiction film such as one of the *Terminator* series expects certain things – time travel, aliens out to destroy the world, heroes who find ways to outwit them, and so on.

Based on an empirical study of a group of female romance readers, Radway explored the circuit by which a certain genre of text was produced, consumed by a specific sort of audience, and finally integrated, though problematically, into the conditions of a lived culture. Radway challenged the notion that the contemporary genre of romance is simply a reflection of the need of some women for fantasy or escape . . . At the center of reading romances is a set of . . . pleasures derived from several sources: the emotional satisfaction of needs often unfulfilled in everyday life, the sense that reading romances is a sort of special gift that women give themselves in creating their own times and spaces, and a sort of utopian protest against the ordinary roles assigned to women in contemporary culture. Radway concluded from her study that a focus on the act of reading rather than simply on the texts suggests that female readers of popular romances, far from passively reproducing the ideological structures of the dominant culture that commercially produces them for mass consumption, actively select among them and appropriate them as occasions for experiencing forms of pleasure involving self-affirmation and transgressions of the limitations of their everyday lives.

Jere Paul Surber, Culture and Critique: An Introduction to the Critical
Discourses of Cultural Studies *(1998: 251–2).*

CHAPTER 7

Janice Radway
Reading the Romance

Janice Radway's *Reading the Romance: Women, Patriarchy, and Popular Literature* complements Michel de Certeau's *The Practice of Everyday Life* very well. Certeau argues that people who read (to which we must add, since we are dealing with the media, "see" and "listen to") texts of all kinds, often subvert them and suggests that there are ways of resisting the hidden imperatives and masked ideologies in such texts. Radway's research, a form of ethnological analysis, focuses its attention on a group of women who read romances and on the uses and gratifications this activity provides for them.

Readers and Reading

Her book was originally published in 1984 and republished in 1991, with a new introduction. This second printing gave her the opportunity to reflect on her research and on the rather remarkable changes that had taken place in the field of literary analysis and cultural studies in the seven years between the two printings. She had started out with the notion of focusing her attention on the texts of romance novels and different ways they might be interpreted, but she discovered that her real subject was the way romance reading was integrated into the lives of her subjects – a group of dedicated readers of romance novels. As she writes (1991: 7):

What the book gradually became, then, was less an account of the way romances as texts were interpreted than of the way romance reading as a form of behavior operated as a complex intervention in the ongoing social life of actual social subjects, women who saw themselves first as wives and mothers.

This kind of research, she adds, was influenced by the Birmingham University Centre for Contemporary Cultural Studies, which pioneered the use of ethnographic "field studies" in the analysis of how people used the mass media.

Many analyses of popular culture texts offer different readings of a text, based on the disciplines and perspectives of scholars making the analyses. There is a wonderful parody of this in Frederick C. Crews' *The Pooh Perplex* (1963). Crews parodies the kind of articles that might be written about Winnie the Pooh by Freudians, Marxists, Jungians, and academics of other critical persuasions. It seems, from her new introduction, that Radway had contemplated offering a variety of textual interpretations, and then decided an ethnographic study of readers of romances made more sense.

There was an interesting problem for her to deal with. There may be many different ways of interpreting a text, but are there any "preferred" readings that a group of women who read romances will make? She offers her answer to this question (1991: 8):

the book argues . . . that whatever the theoretical possibility of an infinite number of readings, in fact, there are patterns or regularities to what viewers and readers bring to texts in large part because they acquire specific cultural competencies as a consequence of their particular social location. Similar readings are produced, I argue, because similarly located readers learn a similar set of reading strategies and interpretive codes that they bring to bear upon the texts they encounter.

So it is the social situation of readers, and their exposure to similar cultural codes, that lead to different readers interpreting a text in a similar matter.

The Smithton Romance Readers

Radway spent some time with a group of dedicated romance readers, friends of a woman named Dorothy "Dot" Evans, who edited a newsletter on romances and worked in a bookstore in Smithton, a place nearly 2,000 miles from New York. Radway conducted a number of sessions with Dot and a number of her best customers, all of which were tape-recorded. She actually lived with Dot for a short period of time and was able to observe the way Dot lived and the role romance novels played in her life. In addition, Radway had a number of questionnaires that the women filled out – which are found in the appendix to her book.

Her experience with the Smithton women led her to conclude that talking to the women and finding out the role these romances played in their lives was essential, and methods of sampling romances and analyzing them were inadequate. As Radway explains (1991: 49):

> The nature of the group's operation suggests that it is unsatisfactory for an analyst to select a sample of romances currently issued by American publishers, draw conclusions about the meaning of the form by analyzing the plots of the books in the sample, and then make general statements about the cultural significance of the "romance."

She adds that the book-publishing industry is making a mistake by focusing on the preferences that all individuals within the group of romance readers have; in trying to please everyone with a kind of "lowest common denominator" romance, they don't please a great many romance readers.

Radway asked her readers why they read romances and got the following answers – shown here in a slightly modified form (1991:61):

To escape from daily problems.
To learn about faraway places and times.
To relax.
To have a fantasy romance like the heroine's.
To have a period of time for myself.
To follow the adventures of a strong, virile hero.
To read stories that are not sad or depressing.

She adds that on her initial visit to the women, in conversations she had with them, they often used the word "escape" to explain their use of romances, but not in the sense of avoiding their responsibilities or anything like that. These books provided an escape from the routines of everyday life for their readers. It seems that the simple act of picking up a book and being able to read it was a source of considerable gratification to these women. This kind of behavior, she adds, is not restricted to women who read romances or to any sex. She mentions Richard Hoggart's work, *The Uses of Literacy* (1992), on English working-class men who also used reading as a means of escape.

The Smithton women also reread their favorite romances during times of stress and it is probably the case that most romance readers reread romances at various times. Readers of romances tend to see their somewhat compulsive reading of these texts as a habit rather than an addiction, a questionable assertion to my way of seeing things. In some romances, Radway adds, there are elements of resistance to male violence and strivings toward independence and self-reliance. There is, ultimately, a utopian hope found in these works that male–female relationships can be managed successfully, which explains why there is a need for happy endings in these books.

The Romance Formula

What exactly is a romance and what are its characteristics? How do romances differ from other narrative texts? To answer this question, Radway offers what is essentially "a Proppian analysis of the romantic plot" (1991: 120). She asked her Smithton readers for a list of their favorite romances and, with 20 of these books in hand, examined them "to determine whether the same sequence of narrative functions can be found in each of these texts." She adds a qualifier to her Proppian analysis (1991: 120):

> a genre is never defined solely by its constitutive set of functions but by interaction between characters and by their development as individuals. As a result, I have assumed further that the romantic genre is additionally defined for the women by a set of characters whose personalities and behaviors can be "coded" or summarized through the course of the reading process in specific ways . . . By pursuing similarities in the behaviors of these characters and by attempting to understand what those behaviors signify to these readers, I have sought to avoid summarizing them according to my own beliefs about and standards for gender behavior.

She summarizes the narrative structure of the typical romance in the list that follows (1991: 134):

1. The heroine's identity is destroyed.
2. The heroine reacts antagonistically to an aristocratic male.
3. The aristocratic male responds ambiguously to the heroine.
4. The heroine interprets the hero's behavior as evidence of a purely sexual interest in her.
5. The heroine responds to the hero's behavior with anger and coldness.
6. The hero retaliates by punishing the heroine.
7. The heroine and hero are physically and/or emotionally separated.
8. The hero treats the heroine tenderly.
9. The heroine responds warmly to the hero's act of tenderness.
10. The heroine reinterprets the hero's ambiguous behavior as the product of a previous hurt.
11. The hero proposes/openly declares his love for/demonstrates his unwavering commitment to the heroine with a supreme act of tenderness.
12. The heroine responds sexually and emotionally.
13. The heroine's identity is restored.

Romances start, then, with a heroine being removed from her family and familiar surroundings; this is an example of Propp's first function, absentation. Other aspects of this list correspond to variations of one sort or another of Propp's 31 functions, including recognition, when the heroine's goodness and beauty are recognized, and wedding, when the heroine is (or will soon be) married.

What Radway's list suggests is that the romance novel is a highly formulaic genre or kind of text, generally involving the theme of changing male behavior from indifference to love, with a number of formulaic sub-genres that vary on the basic romance formula one way or another. On a simple set of basic behaviors or functions, romance writers have been able to write an incredible number of romances. In effect, we can say about these novels they all are "the same old story," just told in different ways with different rather stereotyped characters plugged in at the relevant points.

Another Happy Ending?

At the conclusion of her book, Radway offers some insights about the power individuals and groups of readers have to resist the power of those who control the media. She writes (1991: 222):

If we can learn, then, to look at the ways in which various groups appropriate and use the mass-produced art of our culture, I suspect we may well begin to understand that although the ideological power of contemporary cultural forms is enormous, indeed sometimes even frightening, that power is not yet all-pervasive, totally vigilant, or complete. Interstices still exist with the social fabric where opposition is carried on by people who are not satisfied by their place within it or by the restricted material and emotional rewards that accompany it.

Michel de Certeau would agree with her; there are good reasons to believe that, for one reason or another (including the fact that people often don't interpret texts the way those who create them think they will) people can resist the power of the media. I need only mention what happened in the countries in Eastern Europe dominated by Russia. As soon as people in these countries discovered that the Red Army would not invade them if they threw out the people who were ruling them, despite 40 years of media propaganda, they did so with hardly a second thought.

Write Your Own Romance

Romance writers make millions of dollars selling their novels to addicted women, and perhaps to some men. Radway has suggested that these texts are formulaic and offered a list of things that generally take place in romance novels. To help readers of this book, I have created a table that will make it even easier to write a romance novel. All you have to do is take items from any of the four columns at the first level and mix them with any items from the four columns at the second level and keep doing this until you have exhausted all the levels. Then you just have to write it up as a novel and send it off to an agent and wait for the money to start rolling in.

Janice Radway

Write Your Own Romance

Daphne Witherspoon found herself abandoned and far away from home and in her darkest hour met

1	2	3	4
Lord Randall Cuthbert riding on his great white steed Palomar.	Slade Slick, a riverboat gambler and smoothie, with greased black hair and a drooping mustache. His teeth were bad, also.	The Reverend Homer, a prairie-riding minister from the Church of the Faithful. He was very handsome in his clerical outfit.	Dr. Lance Hobbes, a neurologist, world-famous mountain climber, and writer of important novels and books on psychology.
Who treated her with scorn, thinking her to be a wanton woman from the lower classes.	Who was very kind to her, but only, she thought, because he wanted to have sexual relations with her . . . as with all women he knew.	Who was hostile and said she seemed to be an unbeliever who needed to be saved. He wanted to convert her to his faith and teach her to speak in tongues.	Who said he noticed a slight facial tic, a sign of serious problems. He wanted to take her mountain-climbing in Tibet to help solve her problems.
Then he noticed that she had a 38-inch bust, gorgeous legs, long blonde hair and	Then he said he could find her a nice place to stay in a place near Las Vegas. "The work isn't	Then he said she needed special attention and said she should meet him at a	Then he decided she was too frail to take mountain-climbing, but he noticed her

Continued

1	2	3	4
sparkling blue eyes.	very hard," he said. You just lie around in bed most of the time.	certain church at midnight.	great beauty . . . her 38-inch bust and long blonde hair and sparking eyes
So, he got into a conversation with her and discovered she was very smart and witty. She noticed that he was very handsome.	But she recognized his evil nature and told him she didn't like Las Vegas, or Reno, for that matter.	But she told him she wouldn't do that because she had lost her faith in man and in God, having been abandoned by a man she thought she would marry.	Then she noticed that he was tall, dark and strikingly handsome, and drove a Maserati. She could tell he came from noble stock.
Then he told her she had stolen his heart, he apologized for his callous treatment of her and declared his undying love for her.	Then he asked her whether she had any sisters or friends who looked like her and who were out of work.	Then he said she lacked "the gift of faith" but he could save her. He added that his church allowed many wives and he proposed to her.	Then she noticed that he had a wonderful sense of humor besides being clever and enormously wealthy.
So she became Lady Cuthbert, moved to England to live in a great mansion. Their love grew	At this point she told him to speak with Rev. Homer Nesbitt, who could save his soul. She decided to go to	But she rejected him, saying she believed in monogamy. He decided to get an MBA and marry a clever	So she became Mrs. Hobbes. They bought a palatial house in Los Angeles and he gave her a Rolls Royce

1	2	3	4
deeper with every day.	Hollywood and become a star and find true love.	executive and live happily ever after.	as a symbol of his undying love.

The essential characteristic of the computer and thus of digital environments, according to Murray, is the ability to execute a series of rules. The computer models and reproduces patterns; the abilities to write a multilinear plot are there for the taking. Murray introduces the term "procedural authorship" to make clear what writing for computer applications involves: Procedural authorship means writing the rules by which the text appears as well as writing the texts themselves. It means writing the rules for the interactor's involvement, that is, the conditions under which things will happen in response to the participant's actions. There appears a world of narrative possibilities which are realized by the reader/interactor.

The computer's rule-processing power is a new kind of performance machine for the procedural writer. Murray emphasizes that nothing will essentially change about the fact that writing is the conscious selection and ordering of elements. A story is an act of interpretation of the world, rooted in the particular perceptions and feelings of the writer.

This concentration on the role of the author as possibility-bestowing, manipulating, choosing entity is to the point, but it overshadows a number of equally important aspects . . . The best technology in her vision, then, is a transparent one. Her point of departure is that every era with the available technology gives expression to universal stories about a constant human nature. New technology transforms universal stories such that they remain relevant in a new era. The patterns are constant because human experience is constant, and though cultural differences may inflect these patterns differently from one place to another, the basic events out of which we tell stories are the same for all of us.

Arie Altena, <www.mediamatic.net/cwolk/view.3190>
downloaded July 11, 2003.

CHAPTER
8

Janet Murray
Hamlet on the Holodeck: The Future of Narrative in Cyberspace

Janet Murray's book takes us from the world of traditional media into the world of cyberspace and holodecks. But if there is a message that lies behind her book it is this – regardless of the techniques available to authors and artists in whatever media they work, in the final analysis, they have to tell good stories.

The Holodeck

She explains what a holodeck is and what it can do. It is very similar in certain ways, if you think about it, to what our brains do when we dream, except that we can turn holodecks on and off at will (1997: 13):

First introduced on *Star Trek: The Next Generation* in 1987, the holodeck consists of an empty black cube covered in white gridlines upon which a computer can project elaborate simulations by combining holography with magnetic "force fields" and energy-to-matter conversions. The result is an illusory world that can be stopped, started, or turned off at will but that looks and behaves like the actual world and includes parlor fires, drinkable tea, and characters . . . who can be touched, conversed with, and even kissed. The *Star Trek* holodeck is a universal fantasy machine, open to individual programming: a vision of the computer as a kind of storytelling genie in the lamp.

The holodeck is a product of the digital age, which Murray suggests begins in the last quarter of the twentieth century. It is the computer, now recognized as more than a device for crunching numbers but as a seemingly all-powerful communication facilitator, that leads to new kinds of stories and new media in which to tell them.

Kinds of Stories

The digital world has opened up to us, "all the major representational formats of the previous five thousand years of human history," she says (1997: 27), and has made it possible to devise new ways to tell stories. Our first stories were linear and episodic in nature, culminating in *Don Quixote*, which she suggests was the first European novel. Later, we developed what she calls "multiform stories" which present a story in multiple versions – versions that are mutually exclusive. She cites a story by Jorge Luis Borges, "The Garden of Forking Paths," written by a character named Ts'ui Pen, as an example of this kind of story. She quotes from the story (1997: 31 quoting 1941: 98):

> In all fiction, when a man is faced with alternatives he chooses one at the expense of the others. In the almost unfathomable Ts'ui Pen, he chooses – simultaneously – all of them. He thus creates various futures, various times which start others that will in their turn branch out and bifurcate in other times.

Borges' story serves as a kind of model for the kinds of narratives that would be created later, using computers, and culminating in video games. She mentions a film that is one of the best examples of this multiform kind of story, the Japanese classic *Rashomon* by Akira Kurosawa (1997: 36–7):

> Multiform stories often reflect different points of view of the same event. The classic example of this genre is *Rashomon* (1950), the Kurosawa film in which the same crime is narrated by four different people: a rape victim; her husband, who is murdered; the bandit who attacks them; and a bystander. The increasing moral confusion of their accounts in part reflects the postwar cultural crisis in Japan.

Janet Murray

This film, I should point out, is often placed in lists of the greatest films ever made. It reflects the influence of a postmodern sensibility on film-makers. It also forces audiences to participate much more actively in making sense of the story and trying to figure out whose account of what happened is the correct one.

Electronic Storytelling

The next step in the development of storytelling took place in the development of electronic media, which developed their own narrative formats and styles. She mentions computer "finger twitch" games such as *Mortal Kombat*, which had very thin narrative lines but elaborate visual environments and ever quicker response times that players found exciting. These games evolved to puzzle games, in which players had to solve certain puzzles to proceed with the game and then to other games that were slower but had more story elements to them. She mentions, as an example, *Myst*. This game, and its sequels, used film techniques to strengthen their dramatic power (1997: 53):

> the CD-ROM game *Myst* (1993) achieves much of its immersive power through its sophisticated sound design. Each of the different areas of the game is characterized by distinctive ambient sounds, like the whistling of wind through the trees or the lapping of waves on the shore, that reinforce the reality of fantasy worlds, which are really just a succession of still images . . . the music track works as a game technique: it provides a clue that I am mouse-clicking along in the right direction . . . But it is not gamelike in tone. Instead, the solemnity of the music reinforces my feeling of having come in immediate contact with a terrible act of depravity. The music shapes my experience into a dramatic scene, turning the act of discovery into a moment of dramatic revelation.

Myst was on one CD-ROM. Its successor, *Riven*, is on five CD-ROMs and is much more elaborate in its storytelling, though it uses the same devices as *Myst*.

Interactive Stories

There are now many different genres of video games and the industry is now larger than the film industry in terms of money spent on players and the various games. These games are all interactive, which means they respond to our inputs and responses to events that take place in them. That is, we participate in the stories and our decisions affect, in various ways, the outcomes. Generally speaking, these stories have a branching structure: At various stages of the game we are faced with choices to make and each choice, in turn, affects other choices we make. Some of them have a maze structure and others a rhizome structure, in which there are connections that can be made between any points in the story. All of these choices have to be programmed into the story, so players have the illusion that their choices really make a difference. In effect, it seems, every choice and its attendant consequences have been placed in the story by the programmers, writers, and artists, who design the story.

Psychologically, these interactive video games "immerse" us in a simulated environment and surround us by another reality, much as swimming in the ocean does, to use Murray's example. In these games we experience the same thing we do when we read novels or see movies, what the writer Samuel Taylor Coleridge described as "the willing suspension of disbelief." This, Murray suggests, is inadequate, for when we are involved with fictions of any kind we do more than suspend disbelief; we create belief. Murray discusses the ideas of the "reader-response" school of literary criticism, which argues that when we read we construct alternative narratives, we adjust the emphasis in the story to suit our own tastes, and we perform the dialogue by the characters in our heads.

In video games we are more active and this provides what she calls "agency," a feeling of satisfaction gained from taking action and seeing the results – in the game – of our decisions and actions. Thus, in adventure video games, we stitch together two important themes: finding a solution to problems and facing what is unknown and frightening. She mentions another genre of video games, journey stories, that take us on quests and involve us in various kinds of activities. Propp would call the protagonists of these games "seeker" heroes.

There are, she suggests, two opposing poles that creators of video games have to navigate: One pole involves pleasure players get from the narrative elements of the game and the other is the pleasure they get from the game-playing, problem-solving, and contest-winning element of the game. Unlike stories, which are told to us, video games require us to participate in the unfolding of the game.

Murray suggests that games give us pleasure three ways – through immersion, through agency, and through transformation. We can transform our-

Janet Murray

selves, thanks to the game, into fighters, cowboys, space heroes, and so on ad infinitum. As she explains (1997: 170):

> storytelling can be a powerful agent of personal transformation. The right stories can open our hearts and change who we are. Digital narratives add another powerful element to this potential by offering us the opportunity to enact stories rather than to merely witness them.
>
> Enacted events have a transformative power that exceeds both narrated and conventionally dramatized events because we assimilate them as personal experiences.

The emotional impact of enactment within an immersive environment is so strong that virtual reality installations have been found to be effective for psychotherapy.

This insight helps explain why the video game industry has grown so remarkably in the last few decades. The gratifications players derive from playing video games – from being immersed in a different world and one of their own choosing, from having a sense of agency and power, and from being able to transform oneself into whatever one wants to be – are so powerful that video games have a strong addictive component to them.

The Same Old Story

In her discussion of narratives, Murray suggests that regardless of the medium, we will be telling variations of the same old stories. She discusses theorists of narration who claim that there are only a limited number of events that can be used in telling stories, and in this respect mentions the work of Ronald B. Tobias, who argues that there are 20 master plots that are found in all literature:

Quest	Adventure	Pursuit	Rescue	Escape
Revenge	The riddle	Rivalry	Underdog	Temptation
Metamorphosis	Transformation	Maturation	Love	Forbidden love
Sacrifice	Discovery	Excess	Ascension	Descent

She also discusses the work of Vladimir Propp and his ideas about functions of characters in stories.

In a sense, then, whatever medium we are dealing with, the stories are, since there are only 20 master plots and 31 functions of characters, more or less the same – it is the differences between the media that make the difference and, in particular, the enabling power of the medium relative to readers, listeners, and players. What new media like video games change, however, is our notion of authorship. When a person is actively involved in affecting the outcome of a story, the line between author and reader, or player, becomes ever fainter. But one question remains – are we talking about authorship or the illusion of authorship, since everything our player-author does has been programmed before hand?

IN
PRACTICE

Hypotheses on *Pac-Man* and Video Games

In the early eighties, when video games were still rather primitive, *Pac-Man* was extremely popular. What follows are some speculations explaining the hidden or unrecognized significance of this video game and video games in general for the American public.

1. *Auto-erotic aspects of video-game playing.*
Electronic media, Marshall McLuhan suggested, can be seen as extensions of ourselves, "outside of our bodies," so when we play these games, we are, so to speak, playing with ourselves. Thus, though the game may be simple and rather banal on the face of things, without stretching the truth too far, it can be seen as a form of electronic masturbation. The fact that we play these games with "joy-sticks" has some symbolic significance here.

2. *Feminized and regressive violence*
In *Pac-Man*, the violence is based on biting and ingestion rather than shooting rockets off and other masculine and phallic forms of aggression. This reflects a feminized form of aggression and a regressive form. We have, from a developmental standpoint, regressed from our phallic stage (*Space Invaders*) to a more infantile oral stage. This might reflect a fear of growing up, of being adults and assuming responsibility, in our young people who played the game. It also might reflect a fear of mature, interpersonal sexuality.

3. The labyrinth metaphor.

Earlier games, of the *Space Invader* genre, involved racing around the universe and zapping aliens with ray guns, rockets, and other similar kinds of weapons. *Pac-Man* takes place in a labyrinth, which suggests that we are trapped and that our possibilities are now limited and bounded. We are no longer free to race around outer space, but have to deal with being confined. This suggests that the American sense of possibility was weak at the time, and that we saw ourselves as prisoners with few possibilities.

4. The dog-eat-dog hypothesis.

A game in which dots eat dots is a metaphor for bourgeois capitalist societies characterized by class conflict and a "dog-eat-dog" mentality. When you are a captive of a labyrinth, and there is no escape, then you can either work toward the collective good or try to maximize things for yourself, and it is this latter goal that is emphasized in *Pac-Man*. *Pac-Man* may reflect a change in the American psyche; the frontier has ended and now, trapped in the labyrinth of America, people are suffering from a loss of nerve and a change of perspective, which makes them focus upon themselves (and how many dots they can gobble).

5. The social, economic, and psychological costs of video games.

My analysis of this game does not accept the commonly held notion that video games are ways of preparing our young people for the new digital age. The newer video games do require some problem-solving, but they also often exact a high psychological and social cost: Many young people who play these games (some of whom become addicted to playing video games) end up with repetitive stress injuries, depressed, alienated from others, antisocial, and obese.

So there's more to video games than fingering a joystick furiously and gobbling up dots or killing aliens.

Language exists on that creative borderzone or boundary between human consciousnesses, between a self and an other. It is this responsive interaction between speakers, between self and other, that constitutes the capacity of language to produce new meaning.

Every utterance generates a response in the other who receives it, even if that response is only within inner speech. However, the initial utterance already anticipates that active response in the receiving other and so shapes itself to take it into account. But neither, of course, was the "initial utterance" actually the first word in any real sense; inevitably its form is moulded not just by the future response but also as "answer" to all relevant previous utterances. This inherently interactive – dialogic – nature of discourse and consciousness (since, as we shall see, consciousness is constituted by language) accounts for the constant generation of new meaning. It also produces a complex understanding of time. Meaning is produced or realized only in the specific utterance of a communication event, that is in a precise historical actualization. However, every utterance is also a responsive link in the continuous chain of other utterances which, in effect, constitute the continuity of human consciousness.

Pam Morris, ed. The Bakhtin Reader: Selected Writings of Bakhtin, Medvedev, Voloshinov (1994: 5).

CHAPTER 9

M. M. Bakhtin
The Dialogic Imagination

Mikhail Bakhtin was born in 1895 and died in 1975. He was exiled by Stalin to Kazakhstan, where he wrote a number of books that are now recognized to be of great importance for literary, and by implication media, criticism and analysis. There is a big controversy about whether he used various aliases for some of his books or whether the people whose names are on these books (Medvedev, Voloshinov) actually wrote them. A Russian scholar I met who knew Bakhtin assured me that Bakhtin did, in fact, write a number of books that were published under other names.

It is only in the last 20 years or so, when his books were translated into English, that Bakhtin's importance has been widely recognized. Some scholars have suggested, in fact, that he is one of the most important thinkers of the twentieth century. Whatever the case, his ideas about carnivalization and dialogical communication have been very influential.

The Importance of the Dialogic

Earlier in this book, in my discussion of theories of comedy, I mentioned Bakhtin's theory of carnivalization – the often wild and orgiastic festivities that took place during medieval carnival periods; there are carnivals still found in Rio, New Orleans, San Francisco, and various other cities throughout the world. This carnivalization has also filtered down into certain aspects of everyday life and informs, for example, much popular comedy.

There is another important theory that Bakhtin developed, which involves the importance of dialogue in communication and in the arts – hence the term "dialogic." When we speak with others, and this takes the form of dialogue, we always keep in mind what has been said earlier in the conversation and we try to anticipate, as best we can, what might be said later in the conversation. As Bakhtin explains (1981: 280):

> The word in living conversation is directly, blatantly, oriented toward a future answer-word: it provokes an answer, anticipates it and structures itself in the answer's direction. Forming itself in an atmosphere of the already spoken, the word is at the same time determined by that which has not yet been said but which is needed and in fact anticipated by the answering word. Such is the situation in any living dialogue.

The opposite of dialogue is monologue, in which we speak to ourselves, or, more commonly, carry on a conversation with ourselves in our own heads. In dialogue, our speech is always oriented toward a listener or a group of listeners. We can say the same about texts in general – works of art such as novels, plays, paintings, sitcoms, police dramas, and soap operas.

Intertextuality

If we take this passage about spoken dialogue and apply it to literary and mass-mediated texts, we find that Bakhtin is suggesting that texts also are affected by the already spoken, or, in this case, already written, produced, created – what you will. As he put it (1981: 53), "every extra-artistic prose discourse – in any of its forms, quotidian, rhetorical, scholarly – cannot fail to be oriented toward the 'already uttered,' the 'already known,' 'the common opinion,' and so on."

What this means is that all works are connected, to varying degrees, or build upon, in various ways, other works and various ideas and notions from the past. Artists, writers, film-makers, musicians – they are all influenced in different ways by previous works by artists, writers, film-makers, and musicians. And they were influenced by those who preceded them. This notion that texts are related to one another is called intertextuality.

M. M. Bakhtin

Bakhtin describes the degree to which authors in the Middle Ages "quoted" other authors, by which he meant made use of their themes, plots, ideas, and characters. As Bakhtin wrote (1981: 69):

> The role of the other's word was enormous at that time; there were quotations that were openly and reverently emphasized as such, or that here half-hidden, completely hidden, half-conscious, unconscious, correct, intentionally distorted, deliberately reinterpreted and so forth. The boundaries between someone else's speech and one's own speech were flexible, ambiguous, often deliberately distorted and confused. Certain types of texts were constructed like mosaics out of the texts of others . . . One of the best authorities on medieval parody . . . states outright that the history of medieval literature and its Latin literature in particular "is the history of appropriation, re-working and imitation of someone else's property" – or as we would say, of another's language, another's style, another's world.

So, in the medieval world, there was much borrowing of one another's material; but the same thing holds true today, because authors (by which I we mean writers of novels, sitcoms, television shows, films, and so on) often share a common set of beliefs and values, a common cultural heritage. Part of this cultural heritage includes familiarity with important works (and sometimes not such important ones) from the past.

This borrowing that Bakhtin writes about is not always done consciously; sometimes it is just a matter of a film director, who has seen films by Hitchcock, for example, using the same kind of shots that Hitchcock tended to use. So some intertextuality is based on style, on ideas, and on types of camera shots, as well as on plots and characters from works in the past. Sometimes this borrowing is done consciously – some symphonic works make explicit use of folk themes, for example. One of the most direct and obvious kinds of borrowing takes place in parody.

Bakhtin on Parody

Textual parody involves a comical and ridiculous imitation of a well-known work. But there are other kinds of parodies as well. One make a parody of a genre, such as the sitcom or the western, and parodies a well-known style. There are many parodies, for example, of Hemingway's literary style, and there's a contest, held annually, for the best Hemingway parody. Bakhtin asserts that every genre has been parodied. He writes (1981: 280):

> It is our conviction that there never was a single strictly straightforward genre, no single type of direct discourse – artistic, rhetorical, philosophical, religious, ordinary everyday – that did not have its own parodying and travestying double, its own comic-ironic *contre-partie*. What is more, these parodic doubles and laughing reflections of the direct word were, in some cases, just as sanctioned by tradition and just as canonized as their elevated models.

With parodies, we have conscious humorous imitations of model texts, genres, and styles, and these imitations were so delightful to people that they honored them as much as the texts and genres that were parodied.

There is a reason for this. It is that people recognized the inherently liberating power of laughter. Bakhtin is most eloquent on this matter (1981: 23):

> As a distanced image a subject cannot be comical; to be made comical it must be brought close. Everything that makes us laugh is close at hand, all comical creativity works in a zone of maximal proximity. Laughter has the remarkable power of making an object come up close, of drawing it into a zone of creative contact where one can finger it familiarly on all sides, turn it upside down, inside out, peer at it from above and below, break open its external shell, look into its center, doubt it, take it apart, dismember it, lay it bare and expose it, examine it freely and experiment with it. Laughter demolishes fear and piety before an object, before a world, making of it an object of familiar contact and thus clearing the ground for an absolutely free investigation of it. Laughter is a vital factor in laying down that prerequisite for fearlessness without which it would be impossible to approach the world realistically.

This is a very important passage, for it suggests that laughter and humor are not ways of escaping from knowing reality but, conversely, ways of getting to know reality and the truth of things. It is laughter, Bakhtin asserts, that abolishes hierarchy and distance – beloved by tyrants – and makes it possible to be realistic about the world. Laughter, Bakhtin adds, "is an extremely important and indispensable step in making possible free, scientifically knowable and artistically realistic creativity in European civilization" (1981:23). We can add all civilizations to this passage, for you find humor and laughter in

CON ON THE COB (BOSTON JOKE)

CONCUPISCENCE

condom

VATICON

YUKON

CONCAVE

SECOND BASEMAN

all societies. It is to parody, the comic form or technique that looms so large in Bakhtin's thinking, that we now turn.

Parody and Laughter	IN PRACTICE

We must distinguish between parody and satire. A parody, as we will understand the term, is generally understood to be a comic imitation of a well-known, identifiable text, genre, or style of writing. If the text, genre, or style cannot be identified, people won't recognize that something is being parodied; they'll take the parody as a humorous work in

Continued

M. M. Bakhtin

its own right, but will not recognize the parodic element of the work. A satire is a comic treatment or ridiculous portrayal of a person or a social institution, but it is not an imitation of a text, style, or genre per se.

Satire relies a great deal upon allusions to stupid things people have said and done, or absurd things we find happening in institutions and in society at large. The basic urge in parody is to imitate, in a ridiculous manner, while the basic urge in satire is to make fun of someone or something. But we often find parodies in satires, so the relationship between the two techniques of humor is complicated. In addition, parodies use various techniques of humor to achieve their effects such as exaggeration, absurdity, and revelation of ignorance. Parodies, we must remember, are humorous imitations and like all humorous works they rely on certain comic techniques.

Woody Allen as a Parodist

Parody is one of the techniques that Woody Allen uses to great effect. Consider, for example, his wonderful parody of a genre — graduation speeches — in his "My Speech to the Graduates" found in his book *Side Effects* (1981: 81):

> More than any other time in history, mankind faces a crossroads. One path leads to despair and utter hopelessness. The other, to total extinction. Let us pray we have the wisdom to choose correctly. I speak, by the way, now with any sense of futility, but with a panicky conviction of the absolute meaninglessness of existence, which could easily be interpreted as pessimism. It is not. It is merely a healthy concern for the predicament of modern man.

Allen is imitating and ridiculing the ponderous, lofty, and self-important style of speeches generally given by famous personages to students at graduating ceremonies. These speeches are usually philosophical in nature and full of "sage" advice on how to be successful in the real world.

Allen offers another spoof of an academic genre – course descriptions found in college catalogues. Here he parodies the style of writing in these descriptions (1978: 43):

INTRODUCTION TO PSYCHOLOGY

The theory of human behavior. Why some men are called "lovely indi-viduals" and why there are others you just want to pinch. Is there a split between mind and body, and, if so, which is better to have? Aggression and rebellion are discussed. (Students particularly interested in these aspects of psychology are advised to take one of the Winter Term courses: Introduction to Hostility; Intermediate Hostility; Advanced Hatred; The-oretical Foundations of Loathing.) Special consideration is given to a study of consciousness as opposed to unconsciousness, with many helpful hints on how to remain conscious.

This parody is successful because Allen captures the terse style of the college catalogue course description while undermining it with false logic and absurdities. As in the parody of the speech to college graduates, he likes to suggest alternatives that sometimes don't make sense or lead to absurd situations. Which is better to have – a mind or a body?

We find parodies in the crazy commercials and ridiculous news broad-cast segments on *Saturday Nite Live* and the news correspondents like Roland Hedley in *Doonesbury*. It's fair to say that parody is one of the most common techniques used by humorists in all media – a comedic workhorse that informs much of our humor.

The tendency to interpret everything in an artistic text as meaningful is so great that we rightfully consider nothing accidental in a work of art . . . Since it can concentrate a tremendous amount of information into the "area" of a very small text (cf. The length of a short story by Cexov [Chekov] and a psychology textbook) an artistic text manifests yet another feature: it transmits different information to different readers in proportion to each one's comprehension; it provides the reader with a language in which each successive portion of information may be assimilated with repeated reading. It behaves as a kind of living organism which had a feedback channel to the reader and thereby instructs him.

Yuri Lotman, The Structure of the Artistic Text *(1977: 23).*

There are two reasons why semiology is a vital area of study for the aesthetics of film. First, any criticism necessarily depends upon knowing what a text means, being able to read it. Unless we understand the code or mode of expression which permits meaning to exist in the cinema, we are condemned to massive imprecision and nebulosity in film criticism, an unfounded reliance on intuition and momentary impressions. Secondly, it is becoming increasingly evident that any definition of art must be made as part of a theory of semiology . . . The whole drift of modern thought about the arts has been to submerge them in general theories of communication, whether psychological or sociological, to treat works of art like any other text or message and to deny them any specific aesthetic qualities by which they can be distinguished, except of the most banal kind.

Peter Wollen, Signs and Meaning in the Cinema *(1972: 16–17).*

CHAPTER
10

Yuri Lotman
Semiotics of Cinema

Yuri (also spelled Jurij) Lotman was a semiotician who taught at Tartu University in Estonia for many years and wrote a number of books dealing with semiotics, culture, and the arts. The "Tartu Group" were semioticians and scholars who were interested in the relationships that existed between language, literature, myth, art and culture, all of which, they suggested, provide models of the world that human beings create to help them make sense of their existence. *Semiotics of Cinema* was published in Russian in 1973 and an English translation was published in 1976 and focuses, as its title suggests, on a semiotic approach to cinema.

Shots, Signs, and the Cinema

Lotman quotes Saussure, who wrote that "In language everything boils down to difference but also to groupings." (1976: 31). This is important because, in the cinema the shot is the basic unit of measurement. As Lotman explains (1976: 23):

> In the cinema world, broken down as it is into shots, there exists the possibility of emphasizing any detail. The shot acquires the kind of freedom inherent in the word. It can be isolated, combined with other

shots according to semantic, rather than natural affinities and groupings, or it can be used in a figurative – metaphoric and metonymic –
sense.

In language, the order of words in a sentence affects the meaning of each
word and of the sentence itself. In the same manner, the order of shots used
in a film affects how viewers interpret the shot and the collection of shots
that forms a scene. These shots can have a literal or "natural" meaning or
can have figurative, that is, metaphoric or metonymic, meanings.

In language we use the term "syntax" which means, roughly speaking,
rules for the ordering of words; in film, there is also a "syntax," namely the
sequence or ordering of shots, and it this sequence of shots that generates
certain meanings in the minds of viewers of a film. Lotman focuses our attention on the fact that every shot conveys meaning because it is, semiotically
speaking, a sign (1976: 31):

Every image on the screen is a sign, that is, it has meaning, it carries
information. This meaning, however, can be of two kinds. On the one
hand, images on the screen reproduce some sorts of objects of the real
world. A semantic relationship is established between these objects and
the screen images. The objects become the meanings of the images
reproduced on the screen. On the other hand, the images on the screen
may be augmented by some additional, often totally unexpected meanings. Lighting, montage, interplay of depth levels, changes of speed,
etc. may impart to the objects additional meanings – symbolic,
metaphorical, metonymical, etc.

The semantic meanings – semantics being the study of meaning in language
– are found, Lotman argues, in shots; the second or semiotic kind of
meaning, involving figurative matters, needs a sequence of shots to generate
meaning.

In general terms, we might think here of the difference between a word
and a sentence, which imparts additional meanings to the words used,
depending upon the order in which they are used.

Everything in a Film has Meaning

At the beginning of this chapter I used a quotation from Lotman's *The Structure of the Artistic Text*, in which he suggested that everything in a work of

art is important. Lotman emphasizes this matter in his discussion of film. He writes (1976: 41):

> Everything which we notice during the presentation of a film, everything that excites and effects us, has meaning. In order to learn how to understand these meanings it is necessary to master the system of meanings, just as we do in the case of classical ballet, symphonic music or any other sufficiently complex, traditional art form.

We bring to the films we see a great deal of outside information that helps us interpret what we see. And the more we know, the more we see. Lotman says "everything we notice," which suggests that we may not notice everything in a film the first time we see it. That would explain why we might find pleasure in seeing films more than once – we notice more the second time we see the film. We see things that had escaped our notice the first time we saw the film, just as when we reread novels we notice things that we missed the first time we read them.

Lotman also suggested that "nothing in a work is accidental." What he meant by this is that the critic of a text – in this case a film, since our concern here is with the semiotics of cinema – must be able to deal with every aspect of a film, which means not only particular shots and sequences of shots, but also music, lighting, sound effects, scenery, pacing, and, of particular importance, considerations of the performance of actors and actresses. This means that film criticism is extremely complicated, since there are so many factors to be dealt with.

For Lotman, it is images of man that are basic. As he writes, "the central place in the world of cinematic 'words' is occupied by images of man. The image brings to cinema an entire world of complex cultural signs" (1976: 43). When you have images of humans on the screen, then you have to consider the significance of various kinds of semiotic signs, such as body types, facial expressions, gestures, body language, fashions, the places where we find people, the things they do, what they say to one another . . . and any number of other matters relating to the way we "read" people and try to make sense of their behavior. All of these matters are affected by the kinds of shots that are used, the sequences of shots, music, sound effects, and other technical matters relating to film.

Film directors tell their stories, Lotman adds, by using three kinds of narration simultaneously – visual, verbal, and musical. To this narration we must add other matters. As Lotman explains (1976: 69):

narration is continually being invaded by sequences of various extra-textual associations

- social, political, historical or cultural
- in the form of allusions . . . Thus narration on a higher level appears as a montage of various cultural models, regardless of which cinematographic means are in order to realize them in the film.

This means that when we see a film we bring to it – just as we bring to any text – all kinds of information, tied to our education, our socio-economic class, and our culture, which we use to interpret what we see in the film and make sense of it. Film viewers, he says, have different levels of preparation.

That raises the question: How do people without a great deal of preparation (or, in some cases, sophistication) make sense of a complex film? Lotman has an answer to this question (1976: 94–5):

The question may arise: how can we reconcile cinematography having great semiotic complexity with the requirements of accessibility and comprehension to a wide segment of viewers having varying degrees of preparation. By its very nature, after all, cinema is a mass medium . . . film is a multi-layered structure, and its layers are organized with unequal degrees of complexity. The audience, having various degrees of preparation, "skims off" various layers of meaning.

This notion, that films (and we can include most texts here) have many layers and that members of audiences "skim off" those layers they can make sense of, has applications for all the mass media as well as work of so-called "elite" culture. It explains why children can enjoy films and television shows that should be too adult or too complicated for them. They "skim off," that is pay attention to, only those layers of these films that they can understand.

This implies that we can find different things in films and other texts each time we see them, and at different stages in our intellectual and emotional level of development. It has been said that you can't step into the same river twice. In the same light, you can see the same film or read the same novel (or experience any complex multilevel text) twice; the text may not have changed but you have.

An Image from the Macintosh "1984" Commercial

Lotman suggests that images in films have many layers of meaning and that the more a person knows, the more a person can "see" in (and can "read" from) an image. The kind of analysis Lotman advocates need not be restricted to films; we can find a great deal of information in photographs, paintings, advertisements, and all kinds of other visual texts.

Interrogating An Image

An image can be taken from any given moment in a film – a particular frame – or any mass-mediated text, such as a shot from a television program. That image in the text cannot be separated from the story itself. Bakhtin's theory of dialogism is relevant here. A given image is part of the "dialogue" of the text; what happens in the image is connected to what happened before it was taken, and what happens afterwards is affected by events shown in the image.

I have chosen an image from the famous Macintosh "1984" commercial because it is a fascinating text and because it is one that is available to everyone on the Internet. This image comes from a commercial that was originally shot in film and then transferred to video. (I learned this from Fred Goldberg, a retired advertising executive who was involved in making the commercial.) So we are dealing with a video image of what was originally a film. The image reproduced here is a photograph of a moment in the commercial rather than a frame from a film, but for our purposes we can consider a still image from a television shot on video and a frame from a film as equivalent.

Ridley Scott, who made the commercial, is a famous director, whose films, such as *Blade Runner* and *Alien,* have been great artistic and commercial successes. His "1984" Macintosh commercial is considered one of the most significant television commercials ever made.

When reading an image, we consider the following topics:

Continued

People in the image	Aesthetic aspects	Intertextual aspects
Age	Design	Relation to other texts
Gender	Lighting	Relation to genres
Body shape, language	Color	Relation to style
Facial expressions	Focus	Allusions to events
Hairstyles, color	Grain	Allusions to people
Props (glasses, jewelry)	Spatiality	Allusions to places
Relationships (implied)	Relation to previous images in text	
Surroundings	Relation to following images in text	
Animals, objects		

With the matters listed in the table in mind, let's consider the "1984" commercial and an image from it.

The "1984" Commercial

One reason this text gained the notoriety it did was because it was such a gripping story full of arresting and remarkable images. Let me offer a brief synopsis of the commercial.

A group of prisoners with shaved heads and heavy, crude boots are shown marching slowly in a gigantic building. There are cuts of a beautiful blonde woman, carrying a small sledgehammer, racing through the building. She is being pursued by guards. The men file into a huge auditorium, where they are then subjected to brainwashing by a man who is shown on a huge television set, spouting gobbledygook. The woman races into the auditorium, hurls the sledgehammer at the screen and smashes it to smithereens, destroying the ability of the man to brainwash the prisoners. They watch in open-mouthed astonishment as the screen explodes. Then a message from Apple Computers is scrolled onto the screen, saying: "On January 24th Apple Computer will introduce Macintosh. And you'll see why 1984 won't be like '1984.'"

This commercial was shown during the broadcast of the 1984 Super Bowl, the only time it was broadcast nationally. But it received so much attention from the press that it was shown any number of times on news shows and other television programs.

An Image from "1984"

The image I have selected shows the blonde woman, running with a large sledgehammer in some kind of a gigantic, futurist auditorium. The prisoners are sitting in the room, staring ahead, their eyes glued to the screen. A shaft of light illuminates the woman. Various round amplifiers are shown on the back wall of the auditorium.

We can "read" this image on a number of different levels:

Literal level: what we see.
Textual level: where it fits in the story or text.
Intertextual level: how the image calls to mind similar images.
Mythic level: how the figures relate to myths.

Continued

I relate this image to these four levels in the table that follows:

Literal	A blonde woman is shown running into a large, futuristic auditorium, carrying a sledgehammer.
Textual	The woman is about to throw her sledgehammer at the huge television image that is brainwashing prisoners.
Intertextual	Calls attention to George Orwell's dystopian or anti-utopian novel, *1984*, and other anti-utopian novels.
Mythic	Recalls the biblical story about how David slew the giant Goliath with a slingshot.

Examining the image and thinking about the woman, her blonde hair, the shaved heads of the prisoners or inmates (or whatever they are), the gigantic size of the auditorium, the lighting, and the color . . . all are signifiers that play an important role in giving the image its meaning. In addition, we can see, then, that an image can have a number of different levels of meaning and each of these different levels contributes, I would suggest, to the power images have to excite us and stir our imaginations. Just as human beings have an unconscious that lurks beneath their consciousness, images also have meanings that are not always immediately apparent. There is more to an image, Lotman reminds us, than meets the eye.

There is no such thing as a good or a bad style. It all depends on how the film maker would have us see his narrative. For Eisenstein, a montage-based style was appropriate for Potemkin; *an expressionistic style was better for* Ivan the Terrible. Potemkin *is concerned with the idea of revolt – the factors that make a society turn on its masters. For that purpose, because it shows contrasts and juxtapositions clearly, montage works well. But for the study of a paranoiac personality, an expressionist style is more appropriate – hence the severe camera angles, long-held shots, and deep shadows of* Ivan.

Charles Eidsvik, Cineliteracy: Film Among the Arts *(1978: 71).*

CHAPTER 11

Sergei Eisenstein
Film Form: Essays in Film Theory

Film Form is a collection of essays written by the great film director, Sergei Mikhailovich Eisenstein, between 1938 and 1945. He was born in 1898 and died in 1948. Although he was then too ill to make any more films, he continued his writing on film theory until the time of his death. Eisenstein made six films in the course of his career. His first, the silent film *The Battleship Potemkin*, was made in 1925, when he was only 27 years old. It brought him worldwide attention and fame. His other films, such as *Alexander Nevsky* and *Ivan the Terrible*, further consolidated his stature as one of the greatest of film-makers.

The Theory of Montage

Eisenstein's notion that montage is the central element in film is one of his best-known theories, and one of the most complicated ones as well. There is a good deal of dispute among film theoreticians about how best to understand or characterize montage. Eisenstein alludes to these disputes in *Film Form*. He mentions that a friend of his, Pudovkin, often visits him late at night and they argue about what montage is (1949: 37):

> A graduate of the Kuleshov school, he [Pudovkin] loudly defends an understanding of montage as a *linkage* of pieces. Into a chain. Again, "brick." Bricks, arranged in series to *expound* an idea.

> I confronted him with my viewpoint of montage as a *collision*. A view that from the collision of two given factors *arises* a concept.

There is a big difference between seeing a film as a linking of shots that suggest an idea to viewers, and a film as a series of collisions that create an emotional response from which a concept or an idea arises.

There are many possible conflicts within a film shot, Eisenstein explains. He lists a number of them (1949: 39):

> *Conflict of graphic directions.*
> *Conflict of volumes.*
> *Conflict of masses. (Volumes filled with various intensities of light.)*
> *Conflict of depths.*

There are other conflicts that occur outside of the single shot:

> *Close shots and long shots.*
> *Pieces of graphically varied directions.*
> *Pieces of darkness and pieces of lightness.*
> *Conflicts between an object and its dimension.*
> *Conflicts between an event and its duration.*
> *Conflicts in sound films between acoustics and optics.*

We see, then, that for Eisenstein, conflicts or differences of one kind or another are the basis of montage. The way a director frames a shot enables him to utilize these elements of montage to create the effects he is seeking. Montage is not, Eisenstein repeats, a matter of placing shots one *after* another, like using blocks to make a building. Montage must always have a "collision" of independent shots, often shots that are opposite one another (as described above), which generate a dramatic response.

A Problem with Montage

One question Eisenstein had trouble explaining was how a concept arises out of a collision. He had written that the basis of every art is conflict and this conflict generated ideas. But how did this work? According to Peter Wollen, in *Signs and Meaning in the Cinema*, he was unable to solve this problem. As Wollen writes (1972: 48–9):

Sergei Eisenstein

Primarily, a work of art remained for him "a structure of pathos," which produced emotional effects in the spectator. The problem was to get the maximum effect. "If we want the spectator to experience a maximum emotional upsurge, to send him into ecstasy, we must offer him a suitable 'formula' which will eventually excite the desirable emotions in him." This was a simple physiological approach; conflict, on various levels and dimensions, on the screen excited emotions in the spectator which would either strengthen his political and social consciousness or jolt him out of his ideological preconceptions to look at the world anew. What baffled Eisenstein was how new concepts could be precisely conveyed. He built up a model, first with four and then with five levels of montage (metric, rhythmic, tonal, overtonal, intellectual), in which, in every case, every level except the last could be described as "purely physiological." The last (intellectual montage) was to direct not only the emotions but "the whole thought process as well."

Eventually, Wollen argues, Eisenstein abandoned his notion that a montage was like a series of explosions in a combustion engine and came to see montage as a fusion of ideas with a focus on overtones in shots, caused by the way they were framed and using associations in people's minds between images and ideas. He also became interested in exploiting the rhythm of shots as well.

Wollen quotes a telling comment by Eisenstein about the Moscow Art Theatre (1972: 65):

> They string their emotions together to give a continuous illusion of reality. I take photographs of reality and then cut them up so as to produce emotions . . . I am not a realist, I am a materialist. I believe that material things, that matter gives us the basis of all our sensations. I get away from realism by going to reality.

The important thing to recognize, Eisenstein asserts, is that by "cutting up" images of reality he is able to create emotional responses in people. And these responses are connected to things, which are the foundation of our sensations, emotions, and ideas.

Ideology and Montage

The question arises – what leads film-makers to put films together the way they do? Eisenstein has argued that cinematography is, in the final analysis, montage; but what informs the work of cinematographers? His answer is that we are all social beings and the social arrangements that obtain in the society where the cinematographer is working – and in particular, the political institutions in that society – are what shapes a cinematographers work. As Eisenstein writes (1949: 3):

> The apparent arbitrariness of matter, in relation to the status quo of nature, is much less arbitrary than it seems. The final order is inevitably determined, consciously or unconsciously, by the social premises of the maker of the film-composition. His class-determined tendency is the basis of what seems to be an arbitrary cinematographic relation to the object placed, or found, before the camera.

Marx had argued, in a famous formulation, that society determines consciousness rather than consciousness determining society. That is, it is the material world – and, in particular, the class system – that shapes consciousness. Eisenstein's position is in keeping with this materialist philosophy. It is class, he suggests, that shapes the way film-makers create their films, from the first shot to the last, even if the film-maker is unaware of this matter. Film-makers work from nature when they make their shots, but their social backgrounds shape the way they put these shots together to create meaning. This also applies, by implication, to the way an author uses words, but in film, it is suggested, the impact is much more powerful, since film-makers have lighting, music, sound-effects, and performers to work with.

IN PRACTICE

Rashomontage

As I pointed out in my discussion of Eisenstein's ideas, there are a number of different interpretations of what montage means. His theory differs from that of another Russian film theorist, Lev Kuleshov, about how to create effects in films. Dennis DeNitto describes Kuleshov's theory in *Film, Form, & Feeling* (1985: 110):

> Kuleshov demonstrated in class experiments that an audience's reactions to an individual shot were influenced by the shots that preceded it and followed it; that is, a cinematic narrative is constructed on the basis of a juxtaposition of related shots. Kuleshov and his associates went further. By imaginative editing and the introduction of images unrelated to but

associatively connected with the narrative, they were able to generate feelings and ideas in a viewer that would not have existed without such creative editing. In short, a series of shots became more than a sum of its parts.

Eisenstein rejected Kuleshov's theory, which was based on linear sequences of shots, and argued that a montage (a French term for "assembly") represented a "collision" of shots, each with different characteristics.

Rashomon and Montage

Let me offer a modification of Eisenstein's theory of montage and suggest that there can also be a collision of narrative elements or accounts of events that generate certain feelings and ideas in viewers. To show this, I will discuss Akira Kurosawa's masterpiece, *Rashomon*, which takes place in twelfth-century Japan. The film was released in 1950 and created a sensation.

In this film a priest, a woodcutter, and another man are shown in Rashomon temple, seeking shelter from a rain storm and discussing strange things that have happened. It seems that a bandit had lured a samurai to a grove where, according to the bandit, valuable swords were to be found. The samurai had left his wife by a stream. The bandit overpowered the samurai and tied him up. Then the bandit ran to the woman and told her that her husband had been bitten by a snake. She accompanied him to the grove, where she found her husband tied up. After a brief battle in which the woman tried to stab the bandit with her dagger, he raped the woman (though there is a question raised as to whether she acquiesced), as her husband looked on. A woodcutter out in the forest stumbled upon the threesome. The husband is dead, but who killed him? At a trial, there follow four different accounts of what happened. The wife claimed that in a trance she killed him. The husband, speaking through a shaman, said that he killed himself with a dagger. The bandit, who has been captured, claims he killed the husband in a fierce sword fight. The woodsman says the bandit killed the husband, who was pleading for his life.

Continued

In Practice

The audience is left with a problem from these accounts, told in a series of flashbacks, of what actually happened in the film. Who is telling the truth? What really happened? The only thing we can be certain of is that the bandit and the samurai's wife had sex. Everything else is questionable.

A Collision of Accounts

The montage effect here stems from a collision of narrative accounts, in addition to aesthetic matters such as the editing of the shots found in the film. *Rashomon* was based on linking two short stories by Ryunosuke Akutagawa (1882–1927), "Rashomon" and "In a Grove." The second story deals with the conflicting accounts of what happened between the samurai, his wife, and the bandit, and the first story serves as a frame for the second story in the film.

These conflicting stories pose a problem: Can we know reality or are we limited to different accounts of reality by those with different ideologies or belief systems? It seems to me that we can consider *Rashomon* to be one of the most important postmodern texts – in the sense that postmodernism questions whether there is a "reality" that we can know in contrast to a perspectivist notion that all we can do is see reality from a given point of view. (Six people standing in a circle around a statue see the statue, but not the whole statue – only what they can see from where they are standing.)

I saw *Rashomon* at a showing at Smith College in 1950. I was absolutely mesmerized by the film and can say that it had an incredible impact upon my life. The problem it raised – about whether we can know reality or even know the truth about anything as simple as what happened between two men and a woman in a grove – has shaped the way I have thought about life, media criticism, and many other things since then. The film moves very slowly but its impact is incredible, for the story – with its collisions of accounts of what happened in a grove – forces us to confront profound questions about the nature of reality, what we can know of it, and what might be called the human condition.

Williams is often interpreted as one of the precursors and key sources of British cultural studies that first emerged in the early 1960s and that has since become a global phenomenon. Developing an expanded conception of culture that went beyond the literary conceptions dominant in the British academy, Williams conceptualized culture as "a whole way of life," that encompasses cultural artifacts, modes of sensibility, values and practices . . . Arguing for the need to think together "culture and society," seeing the importance of media culture, and overcoming the division between "high" and "low" culture, Williams produced an impressive series of publications that deeply influenced the trajectory of British cultural studies.

Meenakshi Gigi Durham *and* Douglas M. Kellner,
Media and Cultural Studies: Key Works *(2001: 114).*

CHAPTER
12

Raymond Williams
Marxism and Literature

We must keep in mind that when we see the word "literature" in this book, we have to expand its definition to involve all the art forms carried by media and not confine ourselves to printed works such as novels, plays, poems, and the like. Williams, in *Marxism and Literature*, concerns himself with "literature" in the broadest sense – that is, also with media and culture in general. As he explains (1977: 136):

> The major modern communications systems are now so evidently key institutions in advanced capitalist societies that they require the same kind of attention . . . that is given to the institutions of industrial production and distribution.

Williams recognized that the media play a central role in modern societies and, as a Marxist critic, he thought they needed to be investigated and analyzed.

He argues that the bourgeois concept of "mass communications" and the allied radical concept of manipulation do not adequately explain the function of the media in society. In the same light, he is not terribly interested in the study of media effects, which, he argues, has preoccupied empirical bourgeois – that is, capitalist – sociology. As he explains (1977: 137):

The complex sociology of actual audiences, highly variable systems (the cinema audience, the newspaper readership, and the television audience being highly distinct social structures), is overlaid by bourgeois norms of "cultural producers" and "the mass public," with the additional effect that the complex sociology of these producers as managers and agents within capitalist systems, is itself not developed.

What is needed, instead, Williams argues, is an analysis of cultural production and distribution – and here we can read mass media as an important component of this cultural production and distribution – and a linking of this to social, economic, and political institutions in a society. It is the interrelationships among the media and a society's institutions that is important.

Signs in Society

There are many different approaches that can be used to make the kind of analyses that will link the media to social and political institutions, and one of the most promising, he suggests, is semiotics. As he writes (1977: 140–1):

For if we have learned to see the relation of any cultural work to what we have learned to call a "sign-system" (and this has been the important contribution of cultural semiotics), we can also come to see that a sign-system is itself a specific structure of social relationships "internally," in that the signs depend on, were formed in, relationships "externally," in that the system depends on, is formed in, the institutions which activate it (and which are then at once cultural and social and economic institutions); integrally, in that a "sign-system," properly understood, is at once a specific cultural technology and a specific form of practical consciousness; those apparently diverse elements which are in fact unified in the material social process. Current work on the photograph, on the film, on the book, on painting and its reproduction, and on the "framed flow" of television, to take only the most immediate examples, is a sociology of culture in this new dimension from which no aspect of a process is excluded.

What this means, then, is that there is a fundamental connection between a sign-system, between the way we learn to interpret signs, and the social and economic institutions in a society that create its signs. And the media, which make use of this sign-system, play a major role in shaping the consciousness of the masses, who consume the films, television shows, and other sign-filled texts carried by the media.

We must remember that Marxists believe that the economic relations in a society, what they call the "base," the economic system found in a country, shapes in profound ways the "superstructure," the cultural institutions and practices and, by extension, the consciousness of individuals in that society. The bourgeoisie own the means of production, including the companies that control the mass media; and they have a petit bourgeoisie, who run these media for them. The workers – what Marx called the proletariat – get their ideas from the media and other institutions controlled or shaped by the bourgeoisie, which is why Marx argued that the ideas of the masses are the ideas of the ruling class.

As Friedrich Engels, who collaborated with Marx on many works, described the relationship between the base and the superstructure in *Socialism: Utopian and Scientific* (in Tucker 1972: 621):

> The new facts made imperative a new examination of all past history. Then it was seen that *all* past history, with the exception of its primitive stages, was a history of class struggles; that these warring classes of society are always the products of the modes of production and exchange, in a word, of the *economic* conditions of their time; that the economic structure of society always furnishes the real basis, starting from which we can alone work out the ultimate explanation of the whole superstructure of juridical and political institutions as well as of the religious, philosophical, and other ideas of a given historical period.

The question arises; Why don't the members of the proletariat – the masses – realize that the ideas they have ultimately come from the ruling class, which wishes to maintain the status quo above everything else. These ideas Marxists describe as "false consciousness." To answer that question, Williams turns to the work of the Italian thinker, Antonio Gramsci (1891—1937), whose theory of hegemonic domination explains things.

Gramsci on Hegemony

Gramsci's use of the term "hegemony" is a rather complicated notion. It is broader than the traditional definition of hegemony, which refers to "political rule or domination, especially in relations between states." Gramsci, Williams says, distinguished between rule, which is expressed in a direct manner and involves coercion, and hegemony, which involves social and cultural matters and relies on convincing people to think certain things and behave in desired ways. As Williams writes (1977: 108):

> For "hegemony" is a concept which at once includes and goes beyond two powerful earlier concepts, that of "culture" as a "whole social process," in which men define and shape their whole lives; and that of "ideology," in any of its Marxist senses, in which a system of meanings and values is the expression or projection of a particular class interest.

We can, if we work hard enough and are alert to the matter, come to recognize ideology in texts (or have this ideology pointed out to us by others), and we can figure out the role of culture as it is related to the economic base. But hegemony, or, more particularly, hegemonic domination, because it is all-pervasive, is difficult to see, to isolate, and to analyze. He explains this phenomenon as follows (1977: 111):

> It is a whole body of practices and expectations, over the whole of living: our senses and assignments of energy, our shaping perceptions of ourselves and our world. It is a lived system of meanings and values – constitutive and constituting – which as they are experienced as practices appear as reciprocally confirming. It thus constitutes a sense of reality for most people in society, a sense of absolute because experienced reality beyond which it is very difficult for most members of the society to move, in most areas of their lives.

Thus hegemony, like a gas that we cannot smell but which can affect us in profound ways, permeates the atmosphere and takes on the guise of the natural. Hegemonic domination, we may say, infiltrates every aspect of everyday life and thus becomes invisible to us.

The question arises: How do people escape from having their minds dominated by the mass media and their consciousness shaped by the ideas of the ruling class, all of this masked by hegemonic domination? If all our knowledge is social, how do we discover this? The answer, some theorists have suggested, is that some people, for one reason or another, become improperly socialized and are able to recognize this hegemony, or as some Marxists describe things, as "ideological hegemonic domination." The people who are able to discern this hegemonic domination then take it upon themselves to educate others about it and help them escape from their false consciousness.

Creativity

Williams concludes his book with a chapter on creativity that relates to one of the themes that we find in a number of our authors – that texts of all kinds are not to be seen simply as reflections of the social order, but have something in them, a spark, that demands attention. He argues that an emphasis on creativity is at the very heart of Marxist thought. But some Marxists, he suggests, have neglected this by "reducing creative practice to representation, reflection, or ideology" (1977: 206). In doing this, Marxism has not made artistic creativity and personal self-creation a part of the ongoing social process. (We will return to the matter of representation in a later chapter in this book.)

This mistake, it is suggested, relegates works of art to nothing but a reflection of various sociological and political concerns. In dealing with the mass media, and, in particular the texts carried by them, we always have to do two things – give these texts their due as creative works and analyze their ideological (in the broadest sense of the term) importance. Postmodernist thinkers, as we shall shortly see, do not accept the difference between works of elite culture and the elite arts and popular culture. This suggests that works of popular culture have certain aesthetic and creative aspects that many people have tended to ignore.

The Prisoner and "The General"

IN PRACTICE

The Prisoner is a cult classic television series that aired for one year (17 episodes) in the late 1960s. In the first episode, "Arrival," the hero of the series, played by Patrick McGoohan, is shown driving through London. He goes to an office, resigns, and returns to his apartment. He is planning a vacation. But he is gassed and awakes in a strange place, "The Village," an island (or so it seems) full of spies who have also been kidnapped and whose names have been taken away from them. Everyone now has a number.

The Prisoner's Arrival

The Prisoner eventually meets a character, Number Two, and the following dialogue takes place:

Continued

> *Prisoner:* Where am I?
> *Number Two:* In the Village.
> *Prisoner:* Who are you?
> *Number Two:* Number Two.
> (In the following episodes it is "The New Number Two.")
> *Prisoner:* Who is Number One?
> *Number Two:* You are . . . Number Six.
> *Prisoner:* I'm not a number. I'm a free man!
> *Number Two.* Hysterical laughter.

Number Six is to try various ways of escaping from the Village, and never succeeds until the last episode, when we finally find out who Number One is (or think we do). Nobody had ever escaped from the Village, we are told, and some who tried aren't always alive when they are brought back.

In each episode there is a new Number Two, who is primarily involved with trying to find out why Number Six resigned and with foiling his attempts to escape from the Village. The series is a brilliant combination of spy story and science fiction and is considered by some to be the most brilliant television drama series ever made.

Countless hours have been spent by fans of the show trying to determine whether the slight pause in Number Two's reply to Number Six's question, "Who's Number One?" which is "You are . . . Number Six" means "You are Number Six" or "You are (in actuality) Number One." We never see Number One until the final episode but he frequently telephones the Number Two characters, often at important times in the stories, and One's presence pervades the series.

"The General"

Every episode of *The Prisoner*, and the series itself, lends itself to many different kinds of interpretation: Freudian, semiotic, sociological, Marxist, and so on. But one episode, "The General," is of particular interest to those interested in a Marxist interpretation of the media. Let me offer a brief synopsis of the episode, which cannot do justice to the symbolism and other aspects of this fascinating text.

In "The General," Number Two, aided by a professor, has devised a method (called "Speedlearn") of imprinting material directly into the cerebral cortexes of anyone who watches a television show. The method is dependent on a super-computer, the General, and the trust people in the Village have in the professor, who created (and hates) the General.

The professor realizes that the General will be used, eventually, to brainwash everyone and is shown running away from the Village on a beach. Before he is captured by Number Two's henchmen, he drops a small tape recorder that Number Six spots and buries in the sand. Later Number Six plays the tape and it warns that Speedlearn is a means of brainwashing people. One member of the administration, Number Twelve (who describes himself as a "cog in the machine"), wants to destroy the General and enlists Six to get into a building where a meeting of the Village's Education Board is going on. Twelve wants Six to send the Professor's warning at the next Speedlearn broadcast. Members of the board and Two all wear dark glasses and are in tails and top hats. Six inserts the Professor's message in a broadcasting device but is caught doing so. Two brings Six and Twelve, whom he suspects of aiding Six, to the room where the General is located and asks the Professor to ask the General who helped Six. Two says he can ask the General a question it can't ask. Two rises to the challenge. Six types a message, the Professor inserts it into the General, which promptly starts self-destructing and starts shocking the Professor, who goes to it to see if he can prevent this from happening. In trying to help the Professor, Twelve is killed, along with the Professor. At the end, Six has destroyed the General and saved the members of the Village from brainwashing.

A Marxist Interpretation of "The General"

In the table that follows I list some basic elements of Marxist analysis and show how these concepts can be used to analyze "The General."

Continued

Alienation.	Everyone on the Island has a number instead of a name. What's worse, everyone acquiesces in this.
Ideas of the ruling class are the ideas of the masses.	Education Board in Top Hats are the shown symbolically as the ruling class. A coin is needed to get into the meeting.
Media are instruments of ruling class and spread false consciousness.	Speedlearn imprints historical information and will imprint ideology directly on everyone's cerebral cortex.
The base and superstructure.	The rulers of the Village are the base and the Education Board is the most essential part of the superstructure.
Hegemonic ideological domination.	Speedlearn is an experiment in directly brainwashing everyone, with no resistance possible.

The Professor, using the General, began his experiment with Speedlearn by teaching everyone in the Village modern European history. After watching a brief television spot, just a few seconds long, everyone in the Village can repeat verbatim what they've learned from the history lesson. Number Two tells Number Six that the history lesson is just a start; soon, Number Two adds, the General will directly imprint on everyone's mind certain ideological notions that Number One wants them to have. Number Six says, "you'll have a row of cabbages" when this is done. Number Two agrees.

When Number Six destroys the General (by asking a question that can't be answered by man or machine – "why?") he saves the people in the Village from being brainwashed by the powers that be in the Village: the never seen (except at the very end of the series) Number One, his deputy, Number Two, and the various members of the education committee, soldiers, guards, technicians and others who are dominated by Number Two.

At the end of the series, in a celebrated – some would say really scandalous – conclusion, we are given ambiguous notions of who or what

Number One is. Number Six, along with a former Number Two who had been killed and then is remarkably brought back to life, and another character escape from the Village, which Number Six destroys.

This episode, which some have seen as a parody of academic life and academic pomp, lends itself to a Marxist analysis, for it deals more than many other episodes in the series with the media and the role the media have in spreading false consciousness to those who consume it. We can contrast Speedlearn, which is most directly found in television commercials, with Slowlearn, which is what education is all about. It would seem that Speedlearn is triumphing and whoever might be a real-life manifestation of Number One is having the last laugh.

"Everyday life" refers to dull routine, the ongoing go-to-work, pay-the-bills, homeward trudge of daily existence. It indicates a sense of being in the world beyond philosophy, virtually beyond the capacity of language to describe, that we simply know as the grey reality enveloping all we do. . . . The "modern world" refers to the products of industrialization and the controls necessary to socialize workers and regulate consumption. It is a society whose rational character is defined through and has its limits set by highly organized groups (bureaucracies) operating through the state and/or the corporate state; whose purpose lies less in production that in consumption; whose level of operation takes place on and is aimed at influencing everyday life. In this way Lefebvre joins together technological, consumer, affluent, and leisure activities empha-sized by other social theorists, into what he calls a society of bureaucratically controlled consumption. Its poetry is found in advertising; its persona is the consumer; and its mechanism for insuring individual conformity lies in the communication of fear – fear of being out of fashion, of not being young and attractive, being odd, out of it, the subtle terrors through which advertising motivates.

Phil Wander, "Introduction."
In Henri Lefebvre, Everyday Life in the Modern World *(1984: vii–viii)*

CHAPTER
13

Henri Lefebvre
Everyday Life in the Modern World

Phil Wander, in the passage quoted above, discusses the two basic components of Henri Lefebvre's *Everyday Life in the Modern World* – his notion of what everyday life is like and his analysis of the dominant social and economic aspects of modern life. On the cover of the Harper Torchbook paperback edition of this book we find a kitchen table on which there is a bowl of cereal, a milk bottle, and a glass of milk. We can look out a window behind these objects and find an explosion of an atom bomb. This image expresses two of the dominants in Lefebvre's thinking. Everyday life is dull, banal, and takes place before a background of compulsion and, ultimately, as we shall see, of terror.

Most of the scholarly analyses of matters related to everyday life, Lefebvre asserts, ignore the ideologies and patterns that lie behind the seeming randomness of all the components of everyday life or what is also called "the quotidian" – such as furniture, objects, news items, timetables, and advertisements. And that is because scholars tend to see the world in terms of their particular interests and fields of concern. In essence, they ignore the big picture. Lefebvre expands on his definition of the quotidian (1971: 24):

> The quotidian is what is humble and solid, what is taken for granted and that of which all the parts follow each other in such a regular, unvarying succession that those concerned have no call to question their sequence; thus it is undated and (apparently) insignificant.

Opposed to the quotidian, Lefebvre suggests, is the modern, which "stands for what is novel, brilliant, paradoxical and bears the imprint of technicality and worldliness; it is (apparently) daring and transitory" (1971: 25). These represent two different sides to a reality that is more amazing than fiction, namely our society, and it is a society that continues to dazzle and confuse us.

The Swarm of Signs

Lefebvre now brings a semiological perspective into his inquiry. He argues that people don't know what to believe and what is signifying what. He writes (1971: 25):

> If you allow the swarms of signs to flow over you from television and radio sets, from films and newspapers, and ratify the commentaries that determine their meanings, you will become the passive victim of the situation; but insert a distinction or two – for instance everyday life and modernity – and the situation is changed: you are now an active interpreter of signs.

What we must do, Lefebrve argues, is allow reason to manifest itself and become critical and analytical – searching for the ideologies hidden in everyday life and the consumer society, which is a major component of the quotidian.

Here Lefebvre moves on to one of the main topics of his book – the role of advertising in society. In France, he points out, market research has focused on specific needs people might have and neglected social needs, especially those relevant to urban existence. He asks (1971: 55):

Does advertising create the need, does it, in the pay of capitalist producers, shape desire? Be this as it may, advertising is unquestionably a powerful instrument; is it not the first of consumer goods and does it not provide consumption with its paraphernalia of signs, images and pattern? Is it not the rhetoric of our society, permeating social languages, literature and imagination with its ceaseless intrusions upon our daily experience and our more intimate aspirations? Is it not on the way to becoming the main *ideology* of our time, and is not this fact confirmed by the importance of propaganda modelled on advertising methods? Has not institutionalized advertising replaced former modes of communication, including art, and is it not in fact the sole and vital mediator between producer and consumer, theory and practice, social existence and political power? But what does this ideology disguise and shape, if not that specific level of social reality we call everyday life, with all its "objects" – clothing, food, furnishing?

Thus, for Lefebvre, advertising has become a dominating force in the contemporary word, an ineluctable power obliterating everything that stands in its way, reshaping culture (including art) and functioning now as the main ideology of ordinary people – an ideology focused on personal consumption and on the satisfaction of personal "needs."

Lefebvre insists on our seeing advertising as a servant of its capitalist producers, which means that advertising plays a dominant role in spreading the false consciousness that mystifies people and convinces them of the justness of the arrangements found in their societies; it is advertising that has created the consumer society and replaced reason and activity with an ideology of consumption. This focus on consumption distracts people from examining their social and political oppression at the hands of the bourgeoisie and prevents them from recognizing their true situation and organizing and taking political action.

From Sign to Signal

There has been, Lefebvre continues, a further development in the domination of everyday life and everyday behavior by advertising; first we shifted from symbols to signs and now signals are replacing signs. He explains (1971: 62):

Though the signal figures in the semantic field together with the symbol and the sign, it differs from these in that is only significance is conventional, assigned to it by mutual agreement . . . The signal commands, controls behaviour and consists of contrasts chosen precisely for their contraction (such as, for instance, red and green); furthermore, signals can be grouped in codes (the highway code is a simple and familiar example), thus forming systems of compulsion.

It is these systems of signals, these codes, that have become the main instruments leading to the domination and manipulation of people. We are now in the Pavlovian world of signal and response – or, as Lefebvre puts it, "the subjection of the senses to compulsions and a general conditioning of everyday life" (1971: 62). These signals come to replace other ways people communicate, other dimensions of language. Ironically, as we become more and more controlled by signals and codes of signals, as compulsion because more widespread, we are fed an ideology telling us that we are more and more liberated. So you have people living under an illusion of freedom – when one of the few freedoms they have is freedom of choice in the consumption of products and services.

Lefebvre continues on with his analysis of the importance of advertising (1971: 107):

It takes possession of art, literature, all available signifiers and vacant signifieds; it is art and literature, it gleans the leavings of the Festival to recondition them for its own ends . . . Publicity [advertising] acquires the significance of an ideology, the ideology of trade, and replaces what was once philosophy, ethics, religion and aesthetics. The time is past when advertising tried to condition the consumer by the repetition of slogans; today the more subtle forms of publicity represent a whole attitude to life; if you know how to choose you will choose this brand and no other . . . you are being looked after, cared for, told how to live better, how to dress fashionably, how to decorate your house, in short, how to exist; you are totally and thoroughly programmed, except that you still have to choose between so many good things.

It is not a pretty picture that Lefebvre paints, and it may be somewhat overblown; and yet his picture of life in consumer societies has a certain resonance, and may help explain the anxiety many people feel and the diffuse sense of alienation that disturbs so many of them. There is a radical disconnection between the compulsion everyone feels in their daily lives – what Lefebvre calls the bureaucratic society of controlled consumption that he argues characterizes modern life – and all the talk about freedom and liberty that we find in these societies. We are fed the illusion that we live in an essentially classless, all middle-class, society – with a few soon-to-be-eliminated pockets of poverty at one end of the spectrum and a dozen or so billionaires at the other.

As an illustration of this I recall listening to a radio program recently about what it means to be rich and hearing a woman whose husband makes a salary of a million dollars a year explaining that she didn't consider her family wealthy and placing herself in the upper middle class. Everything is relative, and she probably compared her family to those of many businessmen who make salaries of 20 or 50 or 100 million dollars a year.

Terrorist Societies

Now Lefebvre's indictment of contemporary capitalist (bourgeois) society moves to a new stage – that of terror. He explains what he means by a terrorist society. Societies characterized by different classes, by extreme poverty on one side and a privileged, exploiting class of people on the other side maintain themselves by two means: ideological persuasion and compulsion, by which he means repression – punishment, laws, courts, the police, armed forces – all of which can use violence to prevent class conflict and violence. These try to convince people that everything is as it should be or they use violent means to repress people.

There is always, he asserts, a conflict between the forces of repression and the forces of evasion of this repression, and that is, in effect, the history of everyday life. Religion plays a role in this repression; when Roman Catholicism could not do an adequate job of keeping the masses repressed, Protestantism stepped in to continue this job. Alluding to Max Weber's work on Protestantism and capitalism, Lefebvre says we must keep in mind the link between the two.

He then characterizes terrorist societies (1971: 147):

> A terrorist society is the logical and structural outcome of an over-repressive society; compulsion and the illusion of freedom converge; unacknowledged compulsion besiege the lives of communities (and of their individual members) . . . In a terrorist society terror is diffuse, violence is always latent, pressure is exerted from all sides on its members who can only avoid it and shift its weight by a super-human effort; each member is a terrorist because he wants to be in power (if only briefly);

thus there is no need for a dictator; each member betrays and chastises himself. Terror cannot be located, for it comes from everywhere and from every specific thing; the "system" (in so far as it can be called a "system") has a hold on every member separately and submits every member to the whole, that is, to a strategy, a hidden end, objectives unknown to all but those in power, and that no one questions.

This analysis takes the notion of hegemonic ideological domination, discussed by Williams, and moves it down from a rather lofty level of abstraction; it makes it more concrete and shows how it operates. It also suggests that this hegemonic domination has a certain power to it that we might not recognize, exerting enormous force on people – a force, that since it cannot be identified and since it comes at them from every direction – is best understood as terror.

Festival and Freedom

Lefebvre's answer to the terrorist society is similar to that implied in Bakhtin's work – festival, as the basis of a permanent cultural revolution. Bakhtin had characterized the battle between the serious and, in Lefebvre's terms, "terrorist" church in the Middle Ages, and the power of laughter and festivity in the common people. Bakhtin's analysis is very similar in nature to that of Lefebvre, and both see festival and the style of life connected with it as the basis for freedom. Lefebvre wants everyday life to become a work of art and wants technology to be devoted to transforming everyday life; creativity no longer is restricted to the work of artists but to ordinary people making their lives a work of art and taking control of their lives and the institutions that govern them.

This notion may sound somewhat utopian, but there are means – as we shall see in our discussion of the work of Michel de Certeau – by which people can resist pressure and find ways to subvert the control of those in power. We live, Lefebvre suggests, in a terrorist society characterized by malaise and endless strife, but there are forces, namely those of laughter, festivity, and carnivalization, described so eloquently by Bakhtin, that people can employ to counter this terror. The battle between these two forces is currently raging and gives those involved in the fight, which includes many people who may not know that they are good soldiers, a certain amount of color and excitement.

Lefebvre talks about the reign of terror that the capitalist world generates in the minds of ordinary people, especially through the realm of advertising and the creation of a consumer culture. The "Living Proof Cream Hydracel" advertisement of Geminesse can be seen, let me suggest, as a graphic example of how corporations terrorize people.

Continued

Consider the way this advertisement, which appeared in *Vogue* magazine, begins. In large print, centered at the top of the page, we read:

> There is
> a fountain of youth.
> It's called water.

Then, underneath, we find the following copy:

> Nature has been telling us this forever. Water keeps a rose fresh and beautiful. A peach juicy. All living things living. Including your skin. The millions of cells in your skin contain water. This water pillows and cushions your skin, making it soft and young-looking. But for a lot of reasons, cells become unable to hold enough water. And the water escapes from your skin. (If you'll forgive us, think of a prune drying up and you'll know the whole story.)

Consider that image – of a juicy peach (a woman when she is young) turning into a dried-up prune (a woman when she is old). Think of the terror women must feel when they think of those two images – of themselves as once "juicy" and "peach-like" and then, as they get older, drying up and become a shriveled and tough prune.

The copywriter then tells readers "the truth" about how moisturizers work: They don't add moisture to skin but keep skin young and soft, not by blocking the escape of water (the way regular moisturizers work) but by helping cellular tissues retain their water. Then the copywriter introduces the product in a personal way. "We are Living Proof by Geminesse. And Our breakthrough is Cream Hydracel," we read.

What we have here is a drama that is being acted out for us. There is a magic potion (we are in the realm of fairy tales and myth now) that pits a heroic warrior – Cream Hydracel – against a group of villains . . . namely regular moisturizers that attempt to block water from escaping from cells but don't help keep it in the cells. The copywriter addresses the reader directly at the end of the advertisement:

Nature gave you a fountain of youth. Cream Hydracel keeps it flowing. The warning is obvious and the reader is left with a horrendous image of water gushing out of her cells, drying her up and making her old, barren, and desert-like, a dried-up old prune. (There is, also, a subtext in the copy about becoming post-menopausal, when a woman's "fountain" has stopped flowing.) These horrors are inevitable, unless a woman uses Geminesse's breakthrough product (we have a hint here of science) which will not only make her skin feel softer but, even better, will make it look younger.

This advertisement can be seen as a kind of fairy tale. Propp would say a heroine is victimized but is able to obtain a magic agent that will enable her to find a prince . . . or keep the one she already has. Lefebvre would say that the unacknowledged compulsions he writes about are most evident in this advertisement, operating here at the cellular level.

We now live in a "recited" society that constantly circulates narratives and stories through the medium of mass communication. In the post-truth world, the consent of the audience, the difference between that explosion of messages that characterizes modernity is no longer stamped with the "authority" of their authors. De Certeau aptly describes the way in which old religious forms of authority have been supplanted by the plurality of narratives that empower the reader, rather than the writer . . . The central paradox of modernity identified by . . . de Certeau is that the more information that is produced by the power bloc, the less it is able to govern the various interpretations made of it by socially situated subjects.

Nick Stevenson, Understanding Media Cultures: Social Theory and Mass Communication *(1995: 91).*

CHAPTER
14

Michel de Certeau
The Practice of Everyday Life

Michel de Certeau's *The Practice of Everyday Life* was published in French in 1974 and in an English translation in 1984. Like Henri Lefebvre's *Everyday Life in the Modern World*, it takes everyday life as its subject, but unlike Lefebvre, Certeau is more optimistic about the possibilities of resistance on the part of ordinary people. Certeau begins his book by mentioning that it developed out of his work on popular culture, and, in particular, of the way people use popular culture. As he explains (1984: xii):

> Many, often remarkable, works have sought to study the representations of a society, on the one hand, and its modes of behavior, on the other. Building on our knowledge of these social phenomena, it seems both possible and necessary to determine the *use* to which they are put by groups or individuals. For example, the analysis of the images broadcast by television (representation) and of the time spent watching television (behavior) should be complemented by a study of what the cultural consumer "makes" or "does" during this time with these images. The same goes for the use of urban space, the products purchased in the supermarket, the stories and legends distributed by the newspapers, and so on.

Certeau raises an interesting question. We know people are exposed to thousands and thousands of images, but do we know what do they do with them?

He offers a suggestion, using an analogy of how indigenous people in countries conquered by the Spanish operated. The Spanish were intent on imposing their own culture on the Indians. and the Indians seemed to acquiesce, but in reality they subverted them by using the rituals and representations to their own ends. The same thing happens, Certeau argues, in contemporary societies where the common people find ways to subvert the culture imposed on them by the "elites." Ordinary people exhibit a creativity in their behavior and ways of making use of the popular culture and mass media that envelops them. The weak have ways, Certeau argues, of making use of the strong.

Strategies and Tactics

Certeau makes a distinction between strategies and tactics. Strategies are employed by those with power and involve the "calculus of force-relationships" that are generally connected to political, economic, and scientific institutions. Tactics, on the other hand, are employed by "the other," by those who are subject to the will and power of organizations and similar entities and have to learn how to seize opportunities and manipulate events for their own purposes and "turn to their own ends forces alien to them." A good analogy here would be those martial arts which turn the power of opponents against them.

This behavior is common to people, as Certeau explains (1984: xix):

> Many everyday practices (talking, reading, moving about, shopping, cooking, etc.) are tactical in character. And so are, more generally, many "ways of operating": victories of the "weak" over the "strong" (whether the strength be that of power people or the violence of things or of an imposed order, etc.), clever tricks, knowing how to get away with things, "hunter's cunning," maneuvers, polymorphic simulations, joyful discoveries, poetic as well as warlike.

So there is a silent but ubiquitous resistance, Certeau asserts, on the part of ordinary people to those forces that seek to dominate them politically, socially, and culturally or, to be more precise, pop culturally and with the mass media.

He offers, as an example, what happens to most people in their everyday lives in contemporary culture. "From TV to newspapers, from advertising to all sorts of mercantile epiphanies, our society is characterized by a cancerous growth of vision" (1984: xxi). This transforms the economy, he adds, into a "semeiocracy," a society dominated by signs and visual images. But what happens is that people who are exposed to all those signs and images find ways of transforming them, "reading" them in their own way, and using them for their own devices. The process is similar in nature to renting an apartment, taking another person's property and transforming it as one pleases.

La Perruque, *"The Wig"*

Certeau offers a concept that describes one of the most common tactics employed by ordinary people – that he calls *la perruque*, which means "the wig." This practice involves workers doing their own work, which seems to be the work of their employers. Nothing of material value is stolen and the worker is on the job. *La perruque* can involve a secretary writing a letter while on company time. Thus workers use company time for their own purposes.

A good example involves workers playing video games on the Internet, sending personal e-mail messages to friends, or buying things on the Internet while in their offices. They are appropriating time from their employers and using it for their own purposes. There is an element of game-playing here and workers find creative ways to outwit their bosses and indulge in pleasurable activities. Despite attempts to repress it, *la perruque*, Certeau suggests, is being practiced more and more. And it is only one example from a repertoire of tricks and ploys that common people use to deal with their bosses and, by implication, those in power in all institutions.

Media Use

These tactics and ploys that people use have implications for the way they relate to the media. Certeau asks an interesting question here (1984: 31):

> Once the images broadcast by television and the time spent in front of the TV set have been analyzed, it remains to be asked what the consumer *makes* of these images and during these hours. The thousands of people who buy a health magazine, the customers in a supermarket, the practitioners of urban space, the consumers of newspaper stories and legends – what do they make of what they "absorb," receive, and pay for? What do they do with it?

These questions are of the utmost importance, for we know that people do not all interpret signs and messages and texts the same way. But most of our theories of the media assume rather passive audiences who let images and stories flow over them and, it is assumed, affect, and perhaps shape, their thinking and behavior.

What Certeau suggests is that there are powerful forces of resistance in people – resistance to political power and to media manipulation. This resistance takes the form of *la perruque* and a repertoire of other kinds of behavior used by the weak to subvert the strong, by those who receive mass-mediated messages to use and manipulate them in their own ways for their own purposes. He proposes a metaphor – the consumer-sphinx – who remains an enigma to everyone involved in the communication process and who employs various tricks to use the mass media for his own purposes.

Certeau uses the term "reading" to deal with how people consume literary works and, by extension, the mass media. He writes (1984: 169):

> Recent analyses show that "every reading modifies its object," that (as Borges already pointed out) "one literature differs from another less by its text than by the way it is read," and that a system of verbal or iconic signs is a reservoir of forms to which the reader must give a meaning . . . The reader takes neither the position of the author nor an author's position. He invents in texts something different from what they "intended." He detaches them from their (lost or accessory) origin. He combines their fragments and creates something unknown in the space organized by their capacity for allowing an indefinite plurality of meanings.

This consumer of the mass media, of verbal and iconic signs, is considerably different from the one characterized by Lefebvre, who assumes that the media have enormous power over people.

There is a debate among media and cultural critics about whether the media are weak or powerful, whether people let the media flow off their backs like water on a duck, or whether the media sink into their feathers (to continue the metaphor) and have profound and long-lasting effects on people. It might be a bit of an oversimplification, but we can say that Lefebvre represents those who believe the media are powerful and Certeau believes the media are weak and that their effects are transitory and not long-lasting, especially since their texts are continually being subverted by their readers and viewers.

Resistance Through Ridicule

Humor is a two-edged sword. It can be used by the powerful to humiliate the weak – members of political, racial, religious, and sexual minorities – but it can also be used by the weak to resist the powerful.

Radio Erevan Jokes

During the years when Russia dominated countries in Eastern Europe, thanks to the power of the Red Army, a number of different kinds of jokes that made fun of socialism, Russians, Marxism, and related subjects sprang up. Human beings have a need, it seems, to turn just about everything, with few exceptions, into a

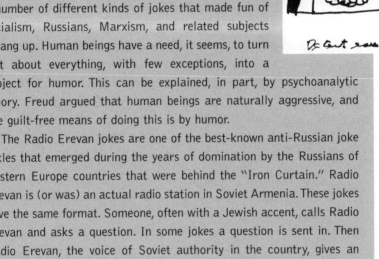

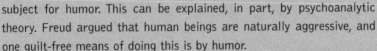

subject for humor. This can be explained, in part, by psychoanalytic theory. Freud argued that human beings are naturally aggressive, and one guilt-free means of doing this is by humor.

The Radio Erevan jokes are one of the best-known anti-Russian joke cycles that emerged during the years of domination by the Russians of Eastern Europe countries that were behind the "Iron Curtain." Radio Erevan is (or was) an actual radio station in Soviet Armenia. These jokes have the same format. Someone, often with a Jewish accent, calls Radio Erevan and asks a question. In some jokes a question is sent in. Then Radio Erevan, the voice of Soviet authority in the country, gives an answer. Let me offer a few Radio Erevan jokes. (I got some of these jokes from Alan Dundes' book, *Cracking Jokes: Studies of Sick Humor Cycles and Stereotypes* [1987], which has chapters on ethnic slurs, elephant jokes, Polish Pope jokes, dead baby jokes, Auschwitz jokes, and jokes from behind the Iron Curtain.)

Joke 1:

> Someone calls Radio Erevan and asks "Would it be possible to import socialism to the Sahara?" "Yes," replies Radio Erevan, but after the first Five-Year Plan, the Sahara will have to import sand.

Continued

The joke pokes fun at the Soviet Five-Year Plans that had all kinds of statistics which, it turns out, bureaucrats made up, and the disastrous economic results of these plans. Thus, if socialist planners come to the Sahara, in five years the Sahara will have to important sand – an incredible absurdity.

Joke 2:

> Someone calls Radio Erevan and asks, "Is it true that Comrade Gorshenko won 5,000 Rubles at the Lottery?" "Yes," replies Radio Erevan. "Except that it was Comrade Trubeskoy and not Comrade Gorshenko, and it wasn't 5,000 rubles but 10,000 rubles, and he didn't win it at the Lottery but lost it gambling."

What's interesting about this joke is the disconnection between Radio Erevan answering "yes" to the question about Comrade Gorshenko and then reversing and contradicting every part of the question. Thus Radio Erevan, and the powers that ran things behind the Iron Curtain, are revealed as liars and frauds. You can't assume that anything they tell you has any validity.

Joke 3:

> Someone calls Radio Erevan and asks "Is it possible to use a glass of water as a means of contraception?" "Yes," replies Radio Erevan.
> "Should it be used before or after sex?" asks the caller. "Instead of," replies Radio Erevan.

Here we find the fraudulent nature of Soviet authority being ridiculed on the matter of sex. It answers "yes" to all questions, we see – even about sex – but its advice leads to people not having sex.

Radio Erevan stands for the power of Russia and the various client governments it installed behind the Iron Curtain. Radio Erevan's answers are all absurd and contradictory. Telling these jokes, and many other anti-Russian jokes as well, enabled people trapped behind the Iron Curtain to laugh at their tormentors. This laughter was a form of psychological liberation and resistance through ridicule that was replaced by real liberation when the Soviet Union fell apart.

McLuhan became frustrated trying to teach first year students in required courses how to read English poetry, and began using the technique of analyzing the front page of newspapers, comic strips, ads, and the like as poems . . . This new approach to the study of popular culture and popular art forms led to his first move towards new media and communication and eventually resulted in his first book, The Mechanical Bride, which some consider to be one of the founding documents of early cultural studies. While the Bride was not initially a success, it introduced one aspect of McLuhan's basic method – using poetic methods of analysis in a quasi-poetic style to analyze popular cultural phenomena – in short, assuming such cultural productions to be another type of poem.

Donald Theall, The Virtual Marshall McLuhan *(2001: 4–5)*.

CHAPTER 15

Marshall McLuhan
Understanding Media: The Extensions of Man

Marshall McLuhan, the celebrated Canadian media theorist – some would say "guru" – was born in 1911 and died in 1980. He was originally a literature professor but became interested in the media and wrote a number of books on media and popular culture. His first book, *The Mechanical Bride* (first published in 1951), was not considered by scholars at the time as a "success" though, as Theall argues in the quotation above, the book can be considered one of the founding works in cultural studies.

His work was always controversial and was not accepted by many academics, who disliked his rather flippant style, his association with advertisers and entertainment media figures, and his use of catchy slogans. After he died, scholars tended to forget about him and his ideas, until the Internet and the new media made people rethink his contributions and recognize their importance.

The question McLuhan asked was this: What if we consider the works of popular culture as "poems" or other forms of literature and use some of the traditional methods of literary criticism to analyze them? For many years, popular culture texts, such as comics, detective novels, science-fiction novels, and most films, were considered "sub-literary" and not worth anyone's serious attention. *The Mechanical Bride* showed that there was a great deal to be learned by taking popular culture and the mass media seriously, even though some "snotty" literature professors and sociologists thought otherwise (and some still do). I can recall being on a panel on the media at Stanford University a number of years ago, when a sociologist from Princeton told me that he "covered" popular culture in a half-hour. The field of media analysis and cultural studies which grew out of seeds planted by McLuhan and a few others suggests that it takes more than 30 minutes to deal with the media and popular culture. It has taken me, personally speaking, 40 years.

Hot and Cool Media

McLuhan is famous for a number of aphorisms and insights about media. One of his most interesting is his suggestion that media can be hot or cool. As he writes in *Understanding Media* (1965: 22–3):

> There is a basic principle that distinguishes a hot medium like radio from a cool one like the telephone, or a hot medium like the movie from a cool one like TV. A hot medium is one that extends one single sense in "high definition." High definition is the state of being well filled with data. A photograph is visually "high definition." A cartoon is "low definition," simply because very little visual information is provided. Telephone is a cool medium, or one of low definition, because the ear is given a meager amount of information. And speech is a cool medium of low definition, because so little is given and so much has to be filled in by the listener. On the other hand, hot media do not leave so much to be filled in or completed by the audience. Naturally, therefore, a hot medium like the radio has very different effects on the user from a cool medium like the telephone.

In this passage McLuhan explains his reasoning behind his classification of media as either "hot" or "cool." Hot media have high definition and extend a single sense, which means it is filled with data. Cool media, on the other hand, have relatively little data and require work on the part of the listener or viewer, as McLuhan's contrast between photographs and cartoons demonstrate.

In the table below, I show examples of various manifestations of McLuhan's hot and cool media:

Hot media	Cool media
High definition	Low definition
Filled with data	Relatively little data
Radio	Telephone
Movie	Television
Advanced countries	Backward countries
City slickers	Rustics
Photograph	Cartoon
Printed words	Speech
Books	Dialogues
Lectures	Seminars

We must expend more effort in using or making sense of texts carried – whether it is a telephone conversation or a television program – by cool media. They demand participation and energy; in a sense, with cool media we have to connect the dots, while with hot media, the dots are all connected for us.

We must remember McLuhan's admonition, at the very beginning of *Understanding Media*, that they are all extensions of man and these extensions, whether of the skin, the central nervous system, the hand, or the foot, affect our entire psychic and social being.

The Global Village

The mechanical age, an age of fragmentation and specialization, has given way to the electronic age, he tells us in the introduction to his book. He writes (1965: 5):

> After three thousand years of specialist explosion and of increasing specialism and alienation in the technological extensions of our bodies, our world has become compressional by dramatic reversal. As electrically contracted, the globe is no more than a village. Electric speed in bringing all social and political functions together in a sudden implosion has heightened human awareness or responsibility to an intense degree. It is this implosive factor that alters the position of the Negro, the teen-ager, and some other groups. They can no longer be contained, in the political sense of limited association. They are now involved in our lives, as we in theirs, thanks to the electric media.

McLuhan, we can see, was able to understand the importance of electronic media. He wrote these words before we had an Internet that made it possible to send messages in an instant to people all over the world and turn the world into an electric mall, among other things.

Now McLuhan's metaphor, which suggests that "the world is a global village," seems so self-evident that it seems strange that people could ever challenge it or consider it overblown and absurd. What our new electronic media have done is to make the world, which had been seen in terms of separate nation-states and other distinct and unconnected entities, into the equivalent of a village. In villages people know one another, are involved in other's lives (sometimes to their dissatisfaction), and everyone in the village is affected by what individuals in the village do.

The outbreak of SARS in the spring of 2003 shows to what extent the world is a global village. If China, where SARS first manifested itself, had admitted that there was an outbreak of a new and contagious disease, and taken the proper steps, it could probably have contained SARS without too much difficulty. But China tried to hide the fact that it had a problem and suddenly, because people can travel all over the world so easily, someone with SARS infected others who, in turn, infected others, and in a short time there was a serious global problem facing the medical community. It isn't possible to keep secrets very well in a real village or, now, in a global one.

"The Medium is the Message"

This is one of McLuhan's most famous aphorisms. By this he means that the important thing about a medium is that it alters, in important ways, the sense ratios of people, and this is more important that the "content" or textual matter carried by the medium. As he explained, "The effects of technology do not occur at the level of opinion or concepts, but alter sense ratios or patterns of perception steadily and without any resistance" (1965: 18).

He expands on this notion later in the book, with a discussion of electric light, which he sees as involving total change and as being pure information (1965: 52):

> If the student of media will but meditate on the power of this medium of electric light to transform every structure of time and space and work and society that it penetrates or contacts, he will have a key to the form of the power that is in all media to reshape any lives they touch. Except for light, all other media come in pairs, with one acting as the "content" of the other, obscuring the operation of both.

The newest media take, for their content, what was in the old media, but what is most important in all media is the way they impact upon our central nervous systems and affect our sense ratios.

In 1965 I had the pleasure of meeting McLuhan. He had come to San Francisco and was being hosted by some advertising executives. I read about his being in San Francisco, called the advertising agency, and was fortunate enough to be invited to meet him. We had a short conversation about the topless phenomenon and other aspects of popular culture. Several years later I asked him if he would be willing to write an introduction to a book I wrote called *The TV-Guided American*. He graciously accepted. The problem he faced was that my book analyzed the social, psychological, and political aspects in a number of important television programs in the seventies and he wasn't interested in textual analyses at all. Somehow he managed to write an introduction, even though my book only paid scant attention to the medium of television per se. I must say that I cannot accept this notion of McLuhan's, which makes analyzing texts carried by any medium irrelevant or, at the most, of secondary importance.

A New Perspective on McLuhan

Donald Theall's remarkable biography of McLuhan, *The Virtual Marshall McLuhan*, does a brilliant job of reinterpreting him and showing a very different side to him than we have previously seen. What Theall shows is that most people never understood McLuhan, and neither did many of the McLuhanites, who latched on to this or that aspect of his thought. The McLuhan Theall writes about was a witty satirist and humorist. Theall quotes a letter from McLuhan to Michael Hornyansky, a Canadian poet and English professor, in which McLuhan describes himself, "Most of my writing is Menippean satire, presenting the actual surface of the world we live in as a ludicrous image" (2001: 63).

Theall suggests, then, and offers a great deal of evidence to support his view that we see McLuhan in a new light. He writes (2001: 66):

> From his insistence on his role as poet, satirist, "pattern watcher," and sci-fi predictor of the future (because of his living in the present and loving the past) capable of major contributions to our understanding of the information society, a new figure of McLuhan emerges which demands his revaluation as a twentieth-century poet and satirist concerned with probing rather than theorizing about communication, culture, and technology in the emerging technoculture.

Theall explains how McLuhan became interested in media and popular culture. He had become frustrated trying to teach first-year students how to analyze English poetry and concluded that applying the critical techniques he had learned at Cambridge University from the Cambridge school of literary interpretation to the front pages of newspapers, to advertisements, and to comic strips, made more sense.

This satirical and poetic strategy, Theall adds, was to inform McLuhan's work for the remainder of his career. Much of *The Mechanical Bride* has to be seen as a parody of the ad styles and pop culture world that McLuhan was investigating – as a critic and not as a media theorist. His interest in popular culture led to him speculating and working on media in general, at a time when work on popular culture and the media had little status in universities and academic circles. But it was McLuhan, the satirist and parodist, who had the last laugh on all the scornful academics who had been so negative about his work.

In Practice: *The Financial Times*

The New York Times *First Page*

The first chapter in Marshall McLuhan's *The Mechanical Bride: The Folklore of Industrial Man* is devoted to the front page of *The New York Times* of April 20, 1950.

McLuhan starts the chapter the way he starts every chapter in the book, by asking some questions and making some perceptive comments in bold type. Some of these follow:

> Why is a page of news a problem in orchestration?
> How does the jazzy, ragtime discontinuity of press items link up with other modern art forms?
> To achieve coverage from China to Peru and also simultaneity of focus, can you imagine anything more effective than this front-page cubism?
> You never thought of a page of news as a symbolist landscape?

He suggests that the front page of *The New York Times* has things in common with the visual techniques of Picasso and the literary techniques of James Joyce and then draws out the implication from this insight, writing (1967: 3):

> Quantum and relativity physics are not a fad. They have provided new facts about the world, new intelligibility, new insights into the universal fabric. Practically speaking, they mean that henceforth this planet is a single city.

Continued

We have here the precursor of McLuhan's famous metaphor about the world being a "global village," which has a much stronger resonance and emotional kick than saying the planet is a city.

The Financial Times

The front page of *The Financial Times* makes this global perspective obvious, describing itself as a "World Business Newspaper" in type directly above its name, which is printed in huge letters at the top of the page. The paper announces its subject – finance and business – as well as its scope in a rather assertive manner. It differs from its more popular competitor, *The Wall Street Journal*, which announces its subject by tying itself to a place, Wall Street in New York, the seat of high finance in the United States.

Time, let me suggest, is a more dynamic concept than place; things happen all the time, and Americans are told, as they grow up, that "time is money." *The Financial Times* has a jazzier and more mixed-up look to it; you can see large color photographs on the front page, as well as advertisements and cartoon-like drawings. On the cover of the November 15, 2002, issue, we see a drawing of Uncle Sam that illustrates an article in its weekend edition on European anti-Semitism. It contrasts with the gray and muted look of *The Wall Street Journal*, which uses colors on the front page but in a very diluted way – as screens to separate certain features from the regular news about business and politics.

The graphic designs of the two papers suggest a difference in mentality. *The Financial Times*, which is a British-owned publication, is less parochial and conservative than the *Wall Street Journal*, which generally has two or three times as many pages each day (full of advertisements) than its rival. What they have in common, aside from small type in the stories, is a global perspective, one that is also found in *The New York Times* and other newspapers. Their focus is on business and as such they can be seen as a kind of anti-agitprop, as mouthpieces and glorifiers of multinational capitalism.

Geographers have suggested that there are various "strip cities" in the United States, such as BosNyWash – Boston, New York, and Washington. When it comes to financial and business news, these two newspapers suggest another strip city, a multinational one: LondNy – London and New York (or NyLond, for American partisans) linked by electronic media and a common passion, the pound, the euro, and the dollar bill.

Jameson claims that each stage of capitalism has a corresponding cultural style. Hence, realism, modernism, and postmodernism are the cultural levels of market capitalism, monopoly capitalism, and multinational capitalism.

In characterizing postmodernism as the cultural dominant of late capitalism, Jameson also employs Raymond Williams' . . . distinction between emergent and dominant cultural forms and provides a more radical account of post-modernism as a historical rupture than do radical postmodernists. . . . In his essay "Postmodernism and Consumer Society," (1983), Jameson states "Radical breaks between periods do not generally involve complete changes of content, but rather the restructuration of a certain number of elements already given; features that were subordinate now become dominant, and features that had been dominant again become secondary." This analysis has the virtue of emphasizing the discontinuous nature of the transition to postmodern cultural forms, while also drawing continuities with what preceded them and contextualizing postmodern developments within the larger framework of capitalism itself.

Steven Best and Douglas Kellner, Postmodern Theory: Critical Interrogations *(1991: 186).*

CHAPTER 16

Fredric Jameson
Postmodernism, or, The Cultural Logic of Late Capitalism

Frederic Jameson is one of the most celebrated theorists of postmodernism, a theory, a philosophical movement – call it what you will – that many scholars suggest has had a profound effect on contemporary American culture and many other cultures as well. The term postmodernism is time-related and suggests something coming after, hence "post," modernism. And what is this modernism that has been, some theorists (but not Jameson) argue, superseded by postmodernism?

On Modernism

In his book *Consumer Culture and Postmodernism*, a British scholar, Mike Featherstone, offers an answer to this question. He argues that for both modernism and postmodernism, culture is the central concept (1991: 7):

> In the most restricted sense, modernism points to the styles we associate with the artistic movements which originated around the turn of the century and which have dominated the various arts until recently. Figures frequently cited are: Joyce, Yeats, Gide, Proust, Rilke, Kafka, Mann, Musil, Lawrence and Faulkner in literature; Rilke, Pound, Eliot, Lorca, Valery in poetry; Strindberg and Pirandello in drama; Matisse,

Picasso, Braque, Cézanne and the Futurist, Expressionist, Dada and Surrealist movements in painting; Stravinsky, Schoenberg and Berg in music . . . There is a good deal of debate about how far back into the nineteenth century modernism should be taken (some would want to go back to the bohemian avant-garde of the 1830s). The basic features of modernism can be summarized as: an aesthetic self-consciousness and reflexiveness; a rejection of narrative structure in favour of simultaneity and montage; an exploration of the paradoxical, ambiguous and uncertain open-ended nature of reality; and a rejection of the notion of an integrated personality in favour of an emphasis upon the de-structured, de-humanized subject.

Students of postmodernism generally suggest that modernism ended around 1960 and since then postmodernism has been the cultural dominant, not, Jameson argues, of a whole new postmodern social order but of what turns out to be a new stage in the evolution of capitalism.

Characterizing Postmodernism

Jameson goes into some detail about ways of characterizing postmodernism by the process of exemplification (1991: 1–2):

The enumeration of what follows, then, at once becomes empirical, chaotic, and heterogeneous: Andy Warhol and pop art, but also photorealism, and beyond it, the "new expressionism"; the moment, in music, of John Cage, but also the synthesis of classical and "popular" styles found in composers like Phil Glass and Terry Riley, and also punk and new wave rock (the Beatles and the Stones now standing as the high-modernist moment of that more recent and rapidly evolving tradition); in film, Godard, post-Godard, and experimental cinema and video, but also a whole new type of commercial film . . . Burroughs, Pynchon, or Ishmael Reed, on the one hand, and the French *nouveau roman* and its succession, on the other, along with alarming new kinds of literary criticism based on some new aesthetic of textuality.

We can see that postmodernism reflects a new sensibility that manifests itself in music, literature, and other arts – both popular and elite. Postmodern architecture, for example, is based on the repudiation of the modernist traditions of monotonous slabs of glass and steel and a very constrained and simplified aesthetic. In postmodern architecture, one finds a number of different styles in the same building, a stylistic eclecticism. For example, Philip Johnson's AT&T building has a Roman colonnade on the street level, a neo-classical middle section, and a Chippendale pediment at the top of the building. Las Vegas is a postmodern city and so, Jameson suggests, are certain parts of Tokyo.

Jameson offers a critique of a celebrated postmodern building, The Westin Bonaventure Hotel in Los Angeles, designed by John Portman. He argues that people become disoriented in its lobby, and this is a signifier of more profound problems related to contemporary consumer cultures. He explains (1991: 43–4):

Given the absolute symmetry of the four towers, it is quite impossible to get your bearings in this lobby; recently, color coding and directional signals have been added in a pitiful and revealing, rather desperate, attempt to restore the coordination of an older space. I will take as the most dramatic practical result of this spatial mutation the notorious dilemma of the shop-keepers on the various balconies: it has been obvious since the opening of the hotel in 1977 that nobody could ever find any of these stores, and unlikely to be as fortunate a second time; as a consequence, the commercial tenants are in despair and all the merchandise is marked down to bargain prices. When you recall that Portman is a businessman as well as an architect and millionaire developer, an artist who is at once and the same time a capitalist in his own right, one cannot but feel that here too something of a "return of the repressed" is involved.

So I come to my principal point here, that this latest mutation in space – postmodern hyperspace – has finally succeeded in transcending the capacities of the individual human body to locate itself, to organize its immediate surroundings perceptually, and cognitively to map its position in a mappable external world. It may now be suggested that this alarming disjunction point between the body and its built environment – which is to the initial bewilderment of the older modernism as the velocities of spacecraft to those of the automobile – can itself stand as the symbol and analogon of that ever sharper dilemma which is the incapacity of our minds, at least at present, to map the great global multinational and decentered communicational network in which we find ourselves caught as individual subjects.

So the design and spatiality of this hotel, and the bewilderment it generates in people staying in it or visiting it, functions, for Jameson, as a telling indictment of multinational capitalism and its capacity to turn people into what he calls a "hypercrowd" that is disoriented and confused.

We can see a number of the differences between modernism and postmodernism in the table that follows:

Topic	Modernism	Postmodernism
Time	1860 to 1960	1960 to present
Writers	Joyce, Mann, Kafka	Pynchon, Burroughs
Artists	Matisse, Picasso, Braque	Andy Warhol, photo-realism
Composers	Stravinsky, Schoenberg	Philip Glass, John Cage
Architects	Le Corbusier, Mies van der Rohe	Philip Johnson, Frank Gehry
Tone	Seriousness	Irony, depthlessness
Capitalist stage	Monopoly capitalism	Multinational capitalism

One of the most important features of postmodernism, Jameson explains, is the effacement of the difference between elite arts and popular culture and the mass media.

Postmodernists, he explains, revel in schlock culture and kitsch. As he writes (1991: 159):

> The postmodernists have, in fact, been fascinated precisely by this whole "degraded" landscape of schlock and kitsch, of TV series and *Reader's Digest* culture, of advertising and motels, of the late show and grade-B Hollywood film, of so-called paraliterature, with its airport categories of the gothic and the romance, the popular biography, the murder mystery and the science fiction or fantasy novel.

This is the world of popular culture and everyday life that Lefebvre and Certeau have written about – the kind of culture the "masses" like, the texts, once called "sub-literary," found in our mass media.

What we must recognize, Jameson adds, is that theorists of the postmodern argue that the new postmodern societies no longer are to be understood in terms of the laws of classical capitalism, emphasizing production and the omnipresent matter of class conflict. What is important to see, he argues, is that every position taken by theorists on postmodernism ultimately is also "at one and the same time, and necessarily, an implicitly or explicitly political stance on the nature of multinational capitalism today" (1991: 3). Marx had argued that all history was class conflict; postmodernists, then, in asserting that we had achieved a new kind of society where class was irrelevant, were attempting to escape from history and, without necessarily recognizing what they were doing, masking or obscuring the hidden ideological imperatives in postmodernism.

Utopian Considerations

In his chapter on "Space," Jameson considers this matter of ideology and postmodernism, with his focus on some utopian impulses found in postmodernism. He cites the notion that postmodernism coincides with the so-called "end of ideologies" theory of the 1950s (1991: 159):

> Utopia . . . poses its own specific problem of any theory of the postmodern and any periodization of it. For according to one conventional view, postmodernism is also at one with the definitive "end of ideologies," a development announced (along with "postindustrial society") by the conservative ideologues of the fifties (Daniel Bell, Lipset, etc.) "disproven" dramatically by the sixties, only to "come true" in the seventies and eighties. "Ideology" in this sense meant Marxism, and its "end" went hand in hand with the end of Utopia, already secured by the great postwar anti-Stalinist dystopias, such as 1984. But "Utopia" in that period was also a code word that simply meant "socialism" or any revolutionary attempt to create a radically different society.

So there is an ideological battle going on, masked, one might say, by the development of postmodernist culture. Ultimately, utopian impulses in the sixties were reflected, Jameson adds, in "the development of a whole range of properly spatial Utopias in which the transformation of social relations and political institutions is projected onto the visions of place and landscape, including the human body" (1991: 160). Spatiality – the way people use space in buildings and works of art – can be seen, then, as a signifier of considerable importance for those who know how to "read" it. His discussion of the Westin Bonaventure Hotel is an example of this.

At the conclusion of his book, Jameson muses on what he has written. He points out that he has attempted to instill a sense of class consciousness in his readers, but a class consciousness of a new kind, reflected, in part, in his account of postmodernism and spatiality. He adds (1991: 418):

> I occasionally get just as tired of the slogan "postmodern" as anyone else, but when I am tempted to regret my complicity with it, to deplore its misuses and its notoriety, and to conclude with some reluctance that it raises more problems that it solves, I find myself pausing to wonder whether any other concept can dramatize the issues in quite so effective and economical a fashion.

Jameson raises an interesting question. Is there a better way of characterizing contemporary American culture than postmodernism? I might point out that some philosophers and social theorists argue that postmodernism is now passé and we are not in a post-postmodern period, though what it should be called – to avoid using postmodernism – is anyone's guess.

A Postmodern Perspective on Madonna

The essay that follows deals with Madonna from a postmodern perspective. I have edited the selection slightly to make it more readable and to reduce the amount of postmodernist jargon as much as possible, though you will see this essay is still somewhat difficult to read and to follow. I also have deleted some material from this scholarly essay that is not immediately relevant to our interest in Madonna.

Perspectives on Madonna

This essay was downloaded from the Internet on May 1, 2003. It was written by Professor O. Barbara Sargeant of the Department of Sociology at the University of Massachusetts in Amherst, Massachusetts.

> "Realities of Paradigm: Expressionism, the subtextual paradigm of narrative and libertarianism."

1. Spelling and dialectic theory.
In the works of Madonna, a predominant concept is the concept of textual consciousness. It could be said that the primary theme of the works of Madonna is not, in fact, discourse, but subdiscourse. The example of expressionism prevalent in Madonna's *Sex* emerges again in *Material Girl*, although in a more neocapitalist sense . . . von Ludwig holds that the works of Madonna are empowering. The subject is contextualized into a presemioticist desublimation that includes art as paradox.

2. Narratives of dialectic.
The main theme of the works of Madonna is a self-falsifying reality. In the works of Madonna, a predominant concept is the distinction between destruction and creation. It could be said that the genre of semantic socialism intrinsic to Madonna's *Erotica* is also evident in *Sex*. The premise of pretextual dialectic theory suggests that sexual identity has objective value.

3. Expressionism and textual predeconstructive theory.
In a sense, in *Erotica*, Madonna affirms semantic socialism; in *Sex*, however, she denies textual predeconstructive theory. The characteristic theme of the works of Madonna is the common ground between sexual identity and language.

Bibliography

Tilton, C. ed. (1995) *Semantic Socialism in the Works of Madonna*. University of Illinois Press.
Reicher, N. F. (1983) *The Vermillion Key: Expressionism and Semantic Socialism*. Cambridge University Press.

Did You Have Problems Reading this Essay?

If you had difficulties understanding this essay there is a reason for it. It is complete nonsense and was generated by something called "The

Continued

Postmodern Generator," which creates essays that seem, at first glance, reasonable, but turn out to be unintelligible. This essay was generated at http://www.elsewhere.org/cgi-bin/postmodern/2538.34689225459 and was downloaded on May 1, 2003.

This article, by a nonexistent professor at a real university, is a parody of postmodernism and the style of writing favored by postmodernist theorists. It calls our attention to the fact that a limited number of philosophers, writers, and concepts is enough to create essays that imitate (and ridicule) the kind of writing found in essays about postmodernism. To create your own postmodernist essays with the postmodernism generator, type in "postmodernism" on a search engine such as Google, and you will find that there are literally hundreds of thousands of websites devoted to postmodernism. A site involving the postmodern generator will probably be on the first page. Every time you click on the postmodern generator, you will get a new essay, and each of these essays will be nonsense.

What matters to people is how they should live with other people. The great questions of social life are "Who am I?" (To what kind of a group do I belong?) and "What should I do?" (Are there many or few prescriptions I am expected to obey?). Groups are strong or weak according to whether they have boundaries separating them from others. Decisions are taken either for the group as a whole (strong boundaries) or for individuals or families (weak boundaries). Prescriptions are few or many, indicating the individual internalizes a large or a small number of behavioral norms to which he or she is bound. By combining boundaries with prescriptions . . . the most general answers to the questions of social life can be combined to form four different political cultures.

Aaron Wildavsky, "Conditions for a Pluralist Democracy, or, Cultural Pluralism means More than One Political Culture in a Country" (1982: 7).

CHAPTER 17

Michael Thompson, Richard Ellis, Aaron Wildavsky
Cultural Theory

The quotation from Aaron Wildavsky's article at the start of this chapter offers an overview of the subject that he and two British professors elaborated in their book *Cultural Theory*. It, in turn, draws upon the work of a British social anthropologist, Mary Douglas, who developed a theory that we can use to understand why individuals, who are members of one or another political culture, like certain mass-mediated popular culture texts. Her theory deals with what she calls grid-group relationships.

The Grid-Group Typology

Douglas's grid-group typology is used by our authors to deal with sociological theory and political cultures, but it also has implications that will be of some use to us in our analysis of taste preferences by media audiences. The authors explain the Grid-Group typology – that is, classification system – that Douglas elaborated. They write (1990: 5):

> She argues that the variability of an individual's involvement in social life can be adequately captured by two dimensions of sociality: group and grid. *Group* refers to the extent to which an individual is incorporated into bounded units. The greater the incorporation, the more indi-

vidual choice is subject to group determination. *Grid* denotes the degree to which an individual's life is circumscribed by externally imposed prescriptions. The more binding and extensive the scope of the prescriptions, the less of life that is open to individual negotiation.

The group dimension involves the extent to which an individual's life is shaped and sustained by membership in a group and can be strong or weak. The grid dimension involves whether there are few or many rules and prescriptions individuals have to obey.

The authors assert an "impossibility theorem" which argues, in effect, that grid-group relationships generate five, and only five, ways of life – which Wildavsky, in earlier work used at the beginning of this chapter, described as political cultures. These are: hierarchy, egalitarianism, individualism, fatalism, and autonomy. The last way of life, autonomy, is based on withdrawing from society and is of little concern to us.

We can see how the grid-group theory works by taking the two dimensions – group membership (weak or strong) and grid aspects (few or many rules and prescriptions) – to show how it generates the four ways of life or political cultures.

Way of life	Group boundaries	Kinds and number of prescriptions
Hierarchy	Strong	Numerous and varied
Fatalist	Weak	Numerous and varied
Egalitarian	Strong	Few
Individualist	Weak	Few

Our authors describe how the grid-group typology generates the four ways of life (1990: 6–7):

Strong group boundaries coupled with minimal prescriptions produce social relations that are egalitarian . . . When an individual's social environment is characterized by strong group boundaries and binding prescriptions, the resulting social relations are hierarchical . . . Individuals who are bound by neither group incorporation nor prescribed roles inhabit an individualistic social context. In such an environment all boundaries are provisional and subject to negotiation . . . People who find themselves subject to binding prescriptions and are excluded from group membership exemplify the fatalistic way of life. Fatalists are controlled from without.

Thompson, Ellis, and Wildavsky

So there are four different ways of life and each of them is in conflict with others, yet all need one another. Hierarchists believe in the need for stratification, but also have a sense of responsibility for those below them; individualists are basically interested in themselves and want the government to protect their freedom to compete with others; egalitarians stress that everyone has the same basic needs and play down differences between people; and fatalists, at the bottom of the totem pole, are bossed around by others and rely on chance and luck to escape from their situation.

Fatalists believe that they are victims of bad luck and are apolitical; individualists stress the importance of limited government, whose primary function, they argue, is to protect private property and stimulate free competition; elitists stress that stratification in society is necessary but also have a sense of obligation towards those below them, unlike the individualists; egalitarians emphasize that everyone has certain needs that must be taken care of (especially the downtrodden fatalists); they tend to oppose mainstream political thought in America.

The authors point out that social scientists are always looking for latent or hidden aspects of social phenomena and use this insight to offer a comment on the Marxist perspective on society (1990: 149):

> Things are never as they seem in class societies, Marx tells us, because exploitation must be disguised for the social order to be sustained. Since rulers do not like to think of themselves as exploiters, benefiting unjustly from the labor of others, and the exploited must be kept ignorant of their subjection lest they revolt, the truth must be kept from both rulers and ruled alike.

The problem, they suggest, is that Marx tied mystification to the capitalist economic system whereas the authors argue that *mystification pervades all ways of life and every aspect of life*, and it is the duty of the social scientist to explore this mystification and explain it. Egalitarians, we can see, are very close to the Marxist position in their focus on treating everyone the same. What Marx didn't realize, our authors assert, is that egalitarianism only functions successfully as a critique of social relationships when it is out of power.

The authors suggest that if Marx had used his formidable powers of analysis to consider egalitarian as well as hierarchist and fatalist (read here "bourgeois" and "proletarian") political cultures, he would have come away with different ideas about revolution and sociopolitical institutions.

In Wildavsky's 1982 essay, he argued that you need all four groups for democracy to flourish in a country, and, in addition, the four groups are dependent upon one another. He argued that the individualists and hierarchists (which he called elitists) are the dominant belief system in America, with the egalitarians functioning as the loyal opposition. People in America may not recognize that they belong to one of these political cultures, or "ways of life" to use the grid-group term, and they may not be able to articulate their beliefs. But their membership in one of these four ways of life plays an important role in how they live.

Ways of Life and Media Preferences

Our authors use the grid-group typology to account for taste, and once again, the tie this matter to social relationships. Taste can be defined as the "things that people prefer." People get their preferences for television shows, films, ideas, political parties, and so on from their involvement with others, that is, their social relationships. The authors quote the children's rhyme about Jack Sprat:

> Jack Sprat could eat no fat,
> His wife could eat no lean.
> And so, between the two of them,
> They licked the platter clean.

The authors suggest that the Sprats' taste preferences were not inborn and inherent in them but were formed as they established their relationship.

This matter of establishing taste preferences based on social relationships becomes the model for understanding why people like what they like. It is the social relationships that are primary and dominant, and shape people's preferences.

It is possible, I would suggest, that each of these "ways of life" or political cultures also represents a distinctive audience for books, radio shows, television programs, films, and other media that reflect their values and beliefs. Psychologists tell us that people seek *reinforcement* in the media for their basic beliefs and values and, at the same time, wish to avoid *cognitive dissonance* – things that attack these beliefs and values. It is logical to assume, then, that they will watch television programs that affirm their core values and avoid ones that attack these values.

Thompson, Ellis, and Wildavsky raise another interesting question related to this matter of preference: Are people free? They write (1990: 13):

Placing people in categories seems to many observers to do violence to the individual. For, they ask, if ways of life act as programs telling people what to prefer and how to behave, aren't individuals little better than automatons, robots, ciphers, mere windup toys moved by unseen hands? Solving the problem of preference formation seems to come at the expense of individual choice.

Plural ways of life, we respond, give individuals a chance for extensive, if finite choice. The existence of competing ways of organizing gives individuals knowledge of other possibilities, and the opportunity to observe how people who live according to these other ways are doing.

It is possible for individuals to move from one way of life to another; in some cases, they are forced to do so – for example, when an individualist who is making a high salary is severely injured and unable to work, he or she ends up, then, in the fatalist camp.

A complication, relative to our concern with the media, is that persons in one "way of life" or political culture may be considering moving to another (as from individualist to egalitarian). Thus the shows they watch on television or the books they read or their favorite songs may reflect an anticipated move to a different "way of life" rather than an attachment to and membership in one of the four "ways of life."

There are, our authors explain, "organizational imperatives created by the interaction of the grid and group dimensions that compel people to behave in ways that maintain their way of life" (1990: 262). We are, after all, social animals and our behavior is affected (but not strictly determined) by the groups to which we belong and the rules and prescriptions we obey. Ultimately, they leave us with an enigma (1990: 270):

Cultural theory insists there are five rational and sustainable solutions to every problem . . . How people choose to live (and the consequences that follow from those choices) is what we take to be the domain of cultural theory.

We are left, then, with a theory that complicates our life, for it asserts that there are five "ways of life" or "political cultures" that exist in all democratic societies, and each of them has answers that are of value. There are many different reasons that can be given to explain behavior preferences, but they all stem from two critical factors: the groups in which people are involved and the number and kind of rules and prescriptions they accept as valid.

Cultural Theory, Media, and Popular Culture

We can take cultural theory, with its four (I've dropped the fifth) political cultures and "ways of life," and use it to gain some insights into people's preferences in the realm of media and popular culture. That is, we can make educated guesses, based on what we know about the four groups, about how members of each group will make choices about what television shows to watch, books to read, and so on.

I have used the four political cultures or "ways of life" in courses I used to teach (before I retired) as the basis of a learning game. I divided my class into groups of three students and asked them to figure out which texts would most likely be favored by each political culture. The chart that follows uses a composite of the student choices with some of my own (with some help from some friends) thrown in to update matters.

Topic	Hierarchist	Individualist	Egalitarian	Fatalist
Songs	God Save the Queen	My Way	We are the World	Que Sera Sera
Films	Top Gun	The Color of Money	Woodstock	
Books	The Prince	Looking Out for #1	I'm Okay, You're Okay	Down and Out in London and Paris
Book genres	History	Businessmen biographies	Self-help	Romance novels
TV shows	Lehrer News Hour	Survivor	American Idol	Smackdown wrestling
TV genres	Nature shows	Private eye	Sitcoms	Local TV news
Magazines	Architectural Digest	Fortune	Mother Jones	Soldier of Fortune

Topic	Hierarchist	Individualist	Egalitarian	Fatalist
Newspapers	New York Times	Wall Street Journal	Daily Worker	
Sports	Polo	Golf	Frisbee	Roller Derby
Games	Chess	Monopoly		Russian roulette
Heroes	G. W. Bush	Jack Welsh	Gandhi	Jim Jones
Heroines	Queen Elizabeth	Ayn Rand	Mother Teresa	Courtney Love
Fashion	Uniforms	Three-piece suit	Jeans	Thrift store

What this table suggests is that the media choices people make, their preferences, are influenced (it would be too strong a term to say "determined") to a considerable degree by their particular political culture or way of life. People in each political culture search for texts and other aspects of popular culture that are congruent with their core values and avoid ones that challenge these values.

We have, then, a new way to understand preferences people make about media. This table also can help people who never thought very much about where they belong, as far as political cultures are concerned, determine to which group or "way of life," they owe their ultimate allegiance. Once they see which songs, films, books, television shows, and so on they prefer, they can see where their allegiances lie in the scheme of things. In some cases, they may be surprised.

"Yearning" is the word that best describes a common psychological state shared by many of us, cutting across boundaries of race, class, gender, and sexual practice. Specifically in relation to the postmodernist deconstruction of "master" narratives, the yearning that wells in the hearts and minds of those whom such narratives have silenced is the longing for critical voice. It is no accident that "rap" has usurped the primary position of R&B music among young black folks as the most desired sound, or that it began as a form of "testimony" for the underclass. It has enabled underclass black youth to develop a critical voice, as a group of young black men told me, a "common literacy." Rap projects a critical voice, explaining, demanding, urging. Working with this insight in his essay "Putting the Pop Back into Postmodernism," Lawrence Grossberg comments: The postmodern sensibility appropriates practices as boasts that announce their own – and consequently our own – existence, like a rap song boasting of the imaginary (or real – it makes no difference) accomplishments of the rapper.

bell hooks, "Postmodern Blackness," Postmodern Culture 1, no.1 (September1990).www.sas.upenn.edu/African_Studies/Articles_Gen/ Postmodern_Blackness_18270.html

CHAPTER
18

bell hooks
Black Looks: Race and Representation

There are two topics that dominate this book about African Americans – race and gender. Bell hooks (she spells her name with lower-case letters; it is a pseudonym for her real name, Gloria Watkins) connects these topics to the media, for it is the media that determine the way dominant stereotypes about women and about African Americans are "represented" to people.

The Power of Representations

On the first page of her book, hooks deals with the difference between the economic gains black people have made and the lack of progress they have made in terms of the way they are seen by others. She writes (1992: 1):

> If we compare the relative progress African Americans have made in education and employment to the struggle to gain control over how we are represented, particularly in the mass media, we see that there has been little change in the area of representation. Opening a magazine or book, turning on the television set, watching a film, or looking at photographs in public spaces, we are most likely to see the images of black people that reinforce and reinscribe white supremacy. Those images may be constructed by white people who have not been

divested of racism or by people of color/black people who may see the
world through the lens of white supremacy – internalized racism.

Thus, black people cannot help but become victimized, in terms of the
way they are represented, whether by white people, who by perpetuating
white supremacist view are racists, or by black people or people of color,
who have, hooks argues, internalized the racism of whites. In both cases, this
racism is unconscious and not recognized.

She explains her interest in media (1992: 5):

In *Black Looks*, I critically interrogate old narratives, suggesting alternative ways to look at blackness, black subjectivity, and, of necessity,
whiteness. While also exploring literature, music, and television, many
of these essays focus on film. The emphasis on film is so central because
it, more than any other media experience, determines how blackness
and black people are seen and how other groups will respond to us
based on their relation to these constructed and consumed images.

It is the images of black people, and the narratives in which they are involved,
she suggests, that give people who are not black notions about what
black people are like. At the same time, they tell black people how they
should think about themselves. Images and narratives, then, have implicit
social and ideological content, even though those who are exposed to
them may not recognize this content. That is why examining the media is so
important.

Tina Turner and Black Female Sexuality

One subject that bell hooks is particularly interested in involves the way black
female bodies have been shown in the media. She suggests that black women
have reacted to these representations in two ways – either by passively absorb-
ing these images or by resisting them. Black women, she points out, have traditionally been seen in racist and sexist iconography as freer and more
liberated than white women, as sexually available, licentious, and in some
ways deviant. She offers Tina Turner as an example of a black singer who
has utilized this image.

There is a disconnection, hooks suggests, between the real Tina Turner,
who was raised with puritanical notions about how women were to behave,

and her "construction" of herself, in the media, as "hot" and sexual. As hooks explains (1992: 67):

> Tina Turner's singing career has been based on the construction of an image of black female sexuality that is made synonymous with wild animalistic lust. Raped and exploited by Ike Turner, the man who made this image and imposed it on her . . . Ike's pornographic fantasy of the black female as wild sexual savage emerged from the impact of a white patriarchal controlled media shaping his perceptions of reality. His decision to create the wild black women was perfectly compatible with prevailing representations of black female sexuality in a white supremacist society.

Though she left Ike after years of subjection to his physical abuse, she kept the image and exploited it for her own purposes. She adopted the "blonde lioness mane" to further her career, not recognizing that it also was an endorsement of white racist views that see blonde hair as the ideal for feminine beauty.

Her song, "What's Love Got To Do With It," reinforces this image of herself as a strong black women who is not interested in romantic love but in sexual pleasure for its own right. As hooks explains (1992: 69):

> When sung by black women singers, "What's Love Got To Do With It" called to mind old stereotypes which make the assertion of black female sexuality and prostitution synonymous. Just as black female prostitutes in the 1940s and 1950s actively sought clients in the streets to make money to survive, thereby publicly linking prostitution with black female sexuality, contemporary black female sexuality is fictively constructed in popular rap and R&B songs solely as a commodity – sexual service for money and power, pleasure is secondary.

This matter of subordinating romantic love and using sex for pleasure made the song particularly attractive to contemporary postmodern culture, hooks adds, since it ultimately equated pleasure with an important element of postmodernism – consumption. There is another side to black female sexuality represented by a different school of singers, such as Aretha Franklin, who link romance and sexual pleasure and who "resist" traditional male stereotypes. And there are film-makers who function in an oppositional mode and who try to portray black women in ways differing from conventional stereotypes. What must be done, hooks asserts, is for black women to find new

---

ways to challenge the dominant racist and sexist ways of representing black women.

Madonna and the Appropriation of Black Sexuality

In her analysis of the Madonna phenomenon, hooks asks, is Madonna a "Plantation Mistress or Soul Sister?" Hooks mentions that a number of white women "stars" use and appropriate black culture as signifiers of their radical chic. They manifest a fascination and an envy of blackness, hooks asserts, but the problem with envy is that it tends to take over and consume its subject for its own purposes. Madonna is a prime example of this kind of exploitation, one that has been imitated by some black singers, who also have "blonde ambition."

Madonna, hooks points out, is not liked by black women, many of whom think she can't sing very well. But they are fascinated by her ability to grab attention and continually recreate herself. As hooks explains (1992:158–9):

> For masses of black women, the political reality that underlies Madonna's and our recognition that this is a society where "blondes" not only "have more fun" but where they are more likely to succeed in any endeavor is white supremacy and racism. We cannot see Madonna's change in hair color as being merely a question of aesthetic choice. I agree with Julie Burchell in her critical work *Girls on Film*, when she reminds us: "What does it say about racial purity when the best blondes have all been brunettes (Harlow, Monroe, Bardot)? I think it says that we are not as white as we think. I think it says that Pure is a Bore." I also know that it is the expressed desire of the non-blonde Other for those characteristics that are seen as the quintessential markers of racial aesthetic superiority that perpetuate and uphold white supremacy. In this sense Madonna has much in common with the masses of black women who suffer from internalized racism and are forever terrorized by a standard of beauty they feel they can never truly embody.

This passage raises an important issue. It suggests that blondes function as "others" for people of color – and it is these "others," we must remember, recalling our discussion of semiotics, who give anything its meaning. White blondes function, then, as powerful reminders to black women of their "otherness," one which creates bitterness and self-hatred, among other things.

What Madonna has done, with great success, is to appropriate black culture – that is, to use it for her own purposes – and, at the same time, mock it and undermine it. Thus, her video "Like a Prayer" suggested that she had broken the ties that bound her to white men (in the best white patriarchal manner) but her relationship with black men was based on her being dominant and choosing relationships. Hooks mentions that most of the commentary about the video focused on its use of Catholic images and neglected the racial ones.

In the final analysis, hooks argues, Madonna works within traditional racist lines (1992: 162–3):

In *Truth or Dare* Madonna clearly revealed that she can only think of exerting power along very traditional white supremacist, capitalistic, patriarchal lines. That she made people who were dependent on her for their immediate livelihood submit to her will was neither charming nor seductive to me or the other black folks that I spoke with who saw the film. We thought t it tragically ironic that Madonna would choose as her dance partner a black male with dyed blonde hair . . . He was positioned as a mirror, into which Madonna and her audience could look and see only a reflection of herself and the worship of "whiteness" she embodies – that white supremacist culture wants everyone to embody.

Thus, hooks asserts, Madonna, in the best tradition of white supremacy and patriarchal (that is, male-dominated) culture, has exploited blackness for her own purposes. It is worth noting that Madonna has made a fortune of more than 300 million dollars in the course of her long and controversial career.

We see in bell hooks a woman committed to an ideological critique of American culture and, by implication, the mass media – since the media are such a part of culture. The title shows where she places her emphases – on visual signifiers of race, namely "black looks" – and the subtitle suggests where she will investigate her subject, namely in the representations made of black men and women in the media. Her concerns with – some might say preoccupation with – race and gender, two subjects that until relatively recently tended to be slighted or downplayed by media critics and cultural analysts, are now much more in vogue. And it is reasonable to suggest that she has played an important role in making these two subjects much more visible and a major consideration, now, in media analysis.

Krazy Kat and Blackness

Krazy Kat is generally considered to be among the greatest American comic strips – along with strips such as *Li'l Abner*, *Dick Tracy*, and *Peanuts*, strips that ran for decades and had huge followings. Gilbert Seldes, an important critic of popular culture, described the strip as follows (1924: 207):

bell hooks

KRAZY KAT

IGNATZ

OFFICER PUPP

> *Krazy Kat,* the daily comic strip of George Herriman is, to me, the most amusing and fantastic and satisfying work of art produced in America today. With those who hold that a comic strip cannot be a work of art I shall not traffic. The qualities of *Krazy Kat* are irony and fantasy.

Seldes wasn't alone in his admiration for the strip. It was a remarkable creation, one that amused and entertained millions of Americans from 1913, when it began, until 1944, when Herriman died.

The Plot of the Strip

The plot of *Krazy Kat* always was the same. It involved a brick-throwing mouse named Ignatz throwing a brick at Krazy Kat, who takes being hit by a brick as a sign of love due to his "racial" memories. In Cleopatra's time, a mouse fell in love with Krazy, the beautiful daughter of Kleopatra Kat, and, on the advice of a soothsayer, threw a brick at her with a love message on it. This act has remained with cats, it is asserted, who take being creased with a brick as a sign of love.

Offissa B. Pupp spent decades trying to prevent Ignatz from "creasing" Krazy with a brick and arresting Ignatz for doing so, though Ignatz is always out of jail the next day, figuring out new ways to hit Krazy

Continued

---

with a brick. We have a bizarre love triangle here: Pupp, a dog, loves Krazy, a cat, who, in turn, loves Ignatz, a mouse – and a married mouse at that. Ignatz is not a meek and mild mouse, but an anarchistic one, a monomaniacal brick-thrower who has no fear of dogs or cats or authority.

Krazy's interpretation of being hit with a brick as a sign of love can be seen as an example of valuing illusion over reality. And Ignatz's willfulness is an example of the American belief in the efficacy of individualism, willpower, and self-reliance against forces trying to hold people accountable. Permeating the strip is the "authenticity" of the characters – who maintain their identities and their convoluted love relationships over the decades. Herriman's drawings were always delightful and his use of language was simply brilliant.

George Herriman and "Racial" Memory

The ironic thing about George Herriman is that he too valued illusion over reality. Many years ago I was asked to write an article on Herriman for a biographical reference work, *The Dictionary of American Biography*. When I sent to New Orleans for material (birth certificates) about Herriman's birth and his parents, I received information that there was a George Herriman, Jr. who was born in 1880 – but both of Herriman's parents were mulattos, people of color. Since I "knew" that Herriman was white, I assumed it was another Herriman. The Herriman who did *Krazy Kat* told people he was Greek, and generally wore a hat when any photographs of him were taken. But the editor of *The Dictionary of American Biography* investigated the matter further and concluded that the Herriman I found was the Herriman of *Krazy Kat*, and was a black man.

It seems most likely that Herriman was a very light-skinned black man who passed as a white person. The fact that he felt it necessary to hide his blackness is a commentary on the pressures put on African Americans, which leads some of them to hide their racial identity. And other African American, as bell hooks has explained so brilliantly, may acknowledge their racial identity, but – for a variety of reasons – act and think like white people.

Like his characters, Herriman, valued "illusion" over reality and was affected, in profound ways, by his race and his racial memory. In an analysis I made of *Krazy Kat* in my book *The Comic-Stripped American*, I suggested that two of the dominant themes in the strip were "the victory of illusion over reality" and "the problem of dominance and submission." These themes, it seems, not only were found in Herriman's strip but also became part of his life.

Stuart Hall . . . a British media scholar, has charged that mainstream American mass communication research celebrates a naïve notion of freedom of choice. He argues that the "choice" being offered media audiences is a constrained, truncated choice, one that is ideologically positioned in ways congruent with capitalism, and has little to do with true democracy. By "proving" that people are influenced by opinion leaders, or by innate psychological "needs," mainstream American research ignores the general ideological context that defines what opinion leaders can and will think, and "needs" are legitimated. . . .

The ideological processes that determine political candidates as well as products are hidden, argue critical scholars. Media influence, for Hall and for neo-Marxist scholars in general, is not in overt "messages" but in the ideological structuring or values and beliefs that shape or constrain the message. Ideology is evidenced in the taken for granted, the assumed, the "common sense" of a situation; it is what is not said, because it "goes without saying." It works by excluding what cannot be imagined or thought because it seems bizarre or absurd or beyond the pale.

Joli Jensen, Redeeming Modernity: Contradictions in Media Criticism
(1990: 153–4).

CHAPTER 19

Stuart Hall

Representation: Cultural Representations and Signifying Practices

This book, edited by Stuart Hall, contains two long essays by Hall on representation in the media: "The Work of Representation" and "The Spectacle of the 'Other'." These chapters offer an excellent introduction to Hall's work and are the subject of this analysis.

Defining Representation

In his introduction to this book, Hall points out that culture is now a dominant concern in the social sciences and that analysts of the media and of culture focus their attention increasingly on the production and transmission of meaning. Culture, he tells us, is not primarily a set of things, such as novels or TV shows or comics, but a set of practices involved in creating and transmitting meanings. This suggests, since things don't have a single, fixed meaning – as Saussure pointed out – that it is people who give things meaning and who find meaning in events and things. Hall mentions Saussure and uses him to develop a theory of representation based, to some degree, on semiotics. It is the relations that exist between things, concepts, and signs that are fundamental to the production of meaning in language (and other forms of communication such as images and stories) and it is the process that links these three phenomena together that is known as representation.

Hall raises the question of how people know how to interpret signs, since their relation to objects is arbitrary. His answer is that there are codes that we learn as we grow up in a culture that tell us how to interpret signs of all kinds – words, images, sounds, and so on. As he writes (1997: 36):

> The underlying argument behind the semiotic approach is that, since all cultural objects convey meaning, and all cultural practices depend on meaning, they must make use of signs; and in so far as they do, they must work like language works, and be amenable to an analysis which basically makes use of Saussure's linguistic concepts . . . his idea of underlying codes and structures, and the arbitrary nature of the sign. Thus, when in his collection of essays, *Mythologies* (1972), the French critic Roland Barthes, studies "The world of wrestling," "soap powders and detergents," "The Face of Greta Garbo," or "the *Blue Guides* to Europe," he brought a semiotic approach to bear on "reading" popular culture, treating these activities and objects as signs, as a language through which meaning is communicated.

So it is meaning that we must be concerned about when we study the media and the way the media represent individuals, groups of people, anyone and anything.

In his essay "The Spectacle of the 'Other,'" Hall turns his attention to representations of race. His focus, he explains, will be on the images that are shown in popular culture and the media that deal with "difference" and "otherness." The question he sets out to investigate is whether there have been changes over the years in these representations.

Race and Representation

Hall reprints the cover of the *Sunday Times Magazine* of October 9, 1988, titled "Heroes and Villains." It shows the 100 meters final race in the 1988 Olympics, in which five black athletes are racing toward the finish line. The Canadian sprinter Ben Johnson is pictured winning the race, being trailed by Carl Lewis and Linford Christie. The story in the magazine, it turns out, was about drug-taking in the Olympics; Johnson was stripped of his gold medal for taking drugs, hence he was both a hero and a villain.

Reading an Image

Hall points out that there are several ways to read this image. There is a denotative or literal meaning to this photo – a picture of the 100 meters final, which shows Ben Johnson winning the race. And there is a connotative meaning to it – involving the drug story and, by implication, a sub-theme of race and difference. The meaning of the image, Hall adds, is very ambiguous and open to many different interpretations. There is no "right" or "wrong" way to interpret this photo.

What people seeing the image have to determine is which meaning does the magazine running it want to dominate or to privilege, what Hall calls a *preferred meaning*. Hall suggests the preferred meaning involves both heroism and villainy, since Johnson's triumph was based on his drug use and thus an example of "villainy." The meaning, in this case, is based on both the image and the text provided by the *Sunday Times Magazine.* Underneath the image of the racers we find, in large white letters, "Heroes and Villains." The captions underneath images or textual material superimposed on them play a major role in determining how people interpret images. So you have to interpret the image and the written language connected to it (or the spoken language in the case of television shows and films) to interpret an image correctly.

Hall offers two different readings of the image. One involves the notion that black people are shown "being good at something, winning *at last!*" The second meaning he suggests reads as follows (1997: 228):

> But in the light of the "preferred meaning," hasn't the meaning with respect to "race" and "otherness" changed as well? Isn't it more something like "even when black people are shown at the summit of their achievement, they often fail to carry it off."

What is important here, Hall asserts, is that the behavior of people who are in minorities is frequently interpreted in this binary form of representation, with complementary polar oppositions such as:

good / bad,
civilized / primitive,
repelling because different / compelling because strange and exotic,

and they are often seen in terms of both of these oppositions at the same time. This is an enigma that he answers by exploring the matter of difference.

Differences Matter

This discussion leads him to deal with the question: Why does difference matter? He offers four answers to this question. His first answer is based on the work of Saussure, who argued that difference is important because it is essential to generating meaning. Saussure had said "In language there are only differences." Without differences, then, meaning cannot exist. Saussure also argued that meaning is relational, which forces us to interpret concepts and images and just about everything in terms of their oppositions. Meaning, Hall reminds us, depends on the difference between opposites.

His second answer to the question involves the work of the Russian linguist and critic Mikhail Bakhtin, who focused on how meaning is connected through a dialogue with people. As Hall explains (1997:235):

> Meaning, Bakhtin argued, does not belong to any one speaker. It arises in the give- and-take between different speakers. "The word in language is half someone else's. It becomes 'one's own' only when . . . the speaker appropriates the word, adapting it to his own semantic expressive intentions: it is from there that one must take the word and make it one's own."

So meaning is created through dialogue with one or more others; that is, it is dialogic, and it is generated by the interplay of our speech and others. The "other," then, is essential to the generation of meaning.

For his third answer to the question, Hall turns to the field of anthropology. He writes (1997: 236):

> Mary Douglas . . . argues that social groups impose meaning on their world by ordering and organizing things into classificatory systems. Binary oppositions are crucial for all classification, because one must establish a clear difference between things in order to classify them.

Problems arise, according to Douglas, when things are assigned to the wrong category or when something fails to fit into any category, such as, for example, mulattos, who are neither black nor white or are both black and white, and thus can't be fit into a stable category. Cultures try to avoid such problems by attempting to purify themselves and creating stable symbolic boundaries. This explains why many cultures react so strongly against "foreigners" and others who transgress boundaries. People from different cultures create problems for these symbolic boundaries, and their difference is both repellent to people and, at the same time, attractive and exciting – since it breaks a taboo and threatens the cultural order.

For his fourth explanation, Hall moves to the field of psychoanalytic theory and the importance of "difference" in people's psyches. His argument is that the "other" here is fundamental to people constructing their identities, with a focus on sexual identity. Freud, he writes, focuses on how people construct and consolidate their definitions of themselves, and the primary consideration here involves how they deal with their Oedipal strivings. (The Oedipus Complex was named after Oedipus, the tragic hero of a Greek myth, who discovers that a man he killed at the junction of two roads was his father, and married a woman whom he later discovers was his mother.)

Freud suggested that at an early age a boy develops an unconscious erotic attraction to his mother and finds his father barring the way to his satisfaction. When the male child discovers that females do not have penises, however, the child (because of what Freud called castration anxiety) identifies with his father and begins forming a male identity. The reverse happens with girls, who identify with their mothers and become feminine. This model, Hall reminds us, has been challenged by many other theorists. What is important for our considerations of difference is that sexuality is introduced into the equation and it is "others" (namely our mothers and fathers) who play a major role in our formation and the creation of our sexual identities.

Fighting Stereotypes

Hall points out that we need to use classification systems to make sense of the world – that is, to see things in terms of "types." For example, we use this kind of thinking to deal with genres in the media – soap operas, romance novels, science-fiction stories, tough-guy detective stories, situation comedies, talk shows, and so on. People don't watch television per se. They watch certain types or kinds of shows. So we're always making sense of things by connecting them to classification schemes and broad categories.

What stereotypes do is take a few easily recognized characteristics of a person or a group of people and reduce everything about them to those perceived traits. Thus stereotypes oversimplify and are reductionistic; in addition, they fix differences between people. It reduces the world to "them" and "us," to what belongs and the "other," to insiders and outsiders. In addition, Hall points out, it takes place where there are gross differences in power, in which the group with power can "define," so to speak, the group out of power and classify them as "other."

Hall/s study of stereotyping of black people shows that it has existed for hundreds of years and still exists, "into the late twentieth century." And these stereotypes have always been contested. He cites, for example, D. W. Griffith's *Birth of a Nation* (1915). This film, which introduced many racial stereotypes, was, he suggests, one of the most influential movies of all time. In this film, amazing as it might seem, it is the Ku Klux Klan that is portrayed as heroic and the savior of the American nation.

In the final analysis, Hall argues, it is political power (and everything that stems from it) that determines how people and things are represented, classified, stereotyped, and made different. There are, he adds, ways of countering this kind of negative stereotyping, due to the fact that images have ambiguous meanings and in some cases, negative stereotypes can be fought with positive ones. But as the work of bell hooks, discussed earlier, suggests, the problems of racism in society and in the media are still with us.

9/11 Images as Representation

The image of those planes, piloted by suicidal terrorists, crashing into the World Trade Center is certainly one of the most memorable and most horrible images ever to be seen on a television screen. Many people who saw this image talked about it as like something from a film or video game since it was inconceivable, up to that time, that anyone would take control of a plane and use it as a guided missile to murder thousands of innocent people. Let me offer here some considerations on 9/11 as representation, on the 9/11 image and some metaphors and other notions that can be connected to it.

Terrorists as an Infection

When I saw the horrific images of the planes, taken over by terrorists, crashing into the towers of the World Trade Building, I thought of the planes functioning like an infection . . . of a virus or some foreign body like a virus infecting a cell – attacking us and making us ill and in some cases killing us. A tiny virus, we know, can kill, relatively speaking, a gigantic human being. The plane was like a virus insinuating itself into a cell and then destroying it and the entire entity. And the terrorists became a very important "other" in the minds of Americans – an "other" tied to people with different skin color and religion, from a different part of the world and a different mentality.

Symbolic Castration

The terrorists, though they undoubtedly were unaware of what they were doing, were attempting to make a symbolic castration of American economic and financial power, as represented by the gigantic towers. Towers, from a psychoanalytic perspective, can be seen as phallic symbols, and destroying them was a kind of castration, an attempt to weaken and demoralize Americans. The only more significant, psychoanalytically speaking, symbolic castration terrorists might attempt would be the Washington Monument, the phallic symbol of the father of our country.

Terrorists as Cancer

The language we use about terrorists now suggests that we see them as a kind of cancer. "Sleeper cells" are waiting for the right moment to attack us and, if possible, destroy us. And we all live now like cancer patients – not knowing when seemingly benign cells in our body politic will become activated and cancerous and attack us. We don't know when the next relapse will occur – that is, the next terrorist attack.

In the United States – and all over the world – governments now are hunting down these terrorist cells as best they can, much as doctors operate to cut out cancers in human beings or use chemotherapy or some other method of attack. The fact that we describe these hidden groups of terrorists as being "cells" suggests the appropriateness of the cancer analogy.

Continued

Terrorists as Vermin

We also talk about "cleaning out" and "rooting out" the terrorists in our midst, much as if they were vermin to be found and killed with the human counterpart of bug-killers such as RAID. We have real raids with FBI agents and police trying to discover and neutralize terrorists cells. As a result of 9/11, the American government has undergone a huge reorganization and made defense of the homeland a new priority. We realize that having great oceans on either side of the country doesn't mean anything anymore.

The United States, in our mind's eye, is now like a large mansion whose owners have discovered, suddenly, that it is infected with mold and that all kinds of bugs and other odious creatures have gained entrance. And now, to our great surprise, we've discovered that there are people living in the mansion we didn't know were there.

Aliens Among Us

There is also a science-fiction analogy to be made. There are small groups of people in the United States who believe that extra-terrestrial aliens – from Mars or Venus or some other place in the universe – are living and walking among us . . . and studying us so they can eventually take over the world, enslave us, and do horrible things to us. After 9/11 the fear that aliens are living among us switched from extra-terrestrials to suicidal terrorists from Muslim countries, where Islamic militants trained them – terrorists who are willing to kill themselves when called upon to do so.

We realized, suddenly, that things going on in distant lands like Afghanistan (where people wandered around in costumes that seemed, at first, quite strange to us) could have an impact on us. We went from *War of the Worlds* to a war between modern democratic societies and, as we see things, medieval Islamic fanatics who dream of restoring a kind of Muslim world that never, in fact, existed.

The Irony of 9/11

The irony of 9/11 is that a group of terrorists armed only with box cutters were able to destroy two gigantic buildings, kill more than 3,000 people, shake the American economy, and shock the United States and the world. This tragedy happened in a country that spends more money on its military forces than all other countries in the world combined and is the greatest military power in the world. After 9/11 the world changed. We now worry about terrorists using smallpox or other terrible poisons to kill millions of people . . . and atom bombs too, if they can get their hands on them.

We are all afraid that there will be another attack with even more horrendous images on our television screens. We fear a more destructive attack – one that thousands or even millions of people might not be able to survive – even with the best and most advanced medicine and police and military power there is. The 9/11 images represented a new age – an age of terror that we must all learn to live with.

CHAPTER
20

Afterword
A Confessional

There are some writers who plan out a book in great detail before they start writing it. They know exactly how it will come out before they write the first word. *Making Sense of Media* is not that kind of a book. My mission – not impossible, it turns out, and transmitted not by an audio tape that destroyed itself in a puff of smoke after being played, but by e-mail from my editor – was to write a short primer on some aspects of the media for students taking courses involving the media and for the general public.

My Mission

I chose to write about ideas found in some of the key or foundational texts that many media scholars use when they make their analyses, and other books that I thought are important and deal with subjects that should be addressed.

So this book turned out to be as much a surprise to me as it may be to you. I decided to write a short chapter on each book, but I wasn't sure that my idea would work. I picked a number of books I thought I'd like to write about, but I changed the books on my list as I progressed. When I started on the book I hadn't thought of writing the applications that I wrote for each book. But after I wrote the first few chapters I realized that it would be useful to offer some applications (the sections headed "In Practice"); first I thought of having a section at the back of the book devoted to them but then I decided it was best to write one for each chapter. So, *Making Sense of Media* turned out to be a much more original or personal work than I thought it would be when I started.

There was also the matter of deciding upon the order of chapters. I found, as I wrote the book, that certain books fit nicely together with other books, and so I've arranged them in a way that there would what might be called a "flow," a focus on certain matters or topics that suggested themselves, so to speak. I noticed, with considerable pleasure, that the last essay in this book, by Stuart Hall, mentions the work of the first author in the book, Ferdinand de Saussure, and a number of other authors I deal with, such as Roland Barthes, Mikhail Bakhtin, and Mary Douglas.

A Bit of Humor

I have been interested in humor for many years; I wrote my dissertation on the comic strip *Li'l Abner* and have written a number of books on humor. And, so I've been told, I've got a good sense of humor. So it is only to be expected that I would write some sections of this book that deal with humor or are humorous (or are meant to be humorous). Humor is a liberating force and pervades our media. I think it makes the study of media, which can become overly serious and terribly solemn at times, more palatable.

Communications professors and students generally seem to think that communication is the master discipline that explains and affects everything else, and is central to all other disciplines. Semioticians laugh at this example of hubris, since they *know* that semiotics is the key discipline and everything else is a sub-discipline of it. Semioticians seem so sure of themselves that it gets to be rather irritating at times. So a bit of comedy, for relief, has its virtues, especially since a number of the books in *Making Sense of Media* deal with subjects that lend themselves to a humorous approach. But just because I use humor doesn't mean I'm not serious.

At What Level This Book Might be Used

I hope you found a number of ideas in this book that have stimulated you to think about the media, the texts they carry, and everyday life, in different ways; and I hope you found ideas and concepts that you can use in making your own analyses of our mass-mediated culture. I have written this book in what might be described as "the plain style," the style I use in all my books. I believe in making books as accessible as possible and so I avoid, as much as possible, the kind of scholarly jargon you find in many academic books and journals. Actually, I deal with rather complicated matters in this book, but I have tried to write about them as clearly and simply as I could, so the book has, I think, a depth and complexity that is not immediately apparent.

In the Italian translation of one of my books, a professor from Italy who introduced the book wrote that he thought it would be a good book for students in high school. This struck me as most amusing, as I had met professors at conferences who used the book at every level in college, including graduate seminars. Perhaps, since this book is a primer (one of my books was once described as an introductory primer), if it is translated into Italian, they'll use it in their high schools, perhaps in their equivalent of junior high school?

Whatever the case, whether it is high-school students in Italy or graduate students in the United States, if *Making Sense of Media* helps my readers see the world a bit differently (and perhaps themselves a bit differently) I will consider this book to have been worth the effort involved in writing it.

Bibliography

1. Ferdinand de Saussure, *Course in General Linguistics*

Culler, Jonathan (1975). *Structuralist Poetics: Structuralism, Linguistics, and the Study of Literature*. London: Routledge and Kegan Paul.

Culler, Jonathan (1986). *Ferdinand de Saussure: Revised Edition*. Ithaca, NY: Cornell University Press.

Gottdiener, Mark (1997). *The Theming of America: Dreams, Visions and Commercial Spaces*. Boulder, CO: Westview.

Kevelson, Roberta, ed. (1998). *Hi-Fives: A Trip to Semiotics*. New York: Peter Lang.

Saussure, Fedinand de (1966). *Course in Genral Linguistics*, trans. Wade Baskin. New York: McGraw-Hill.

2. Roland Barthes, *Mythologies*

Barthes, Roland (1972). *Mythologies*, trans. Annette Lavers. New York: Hill & Wang.

Barthes, Roland (1975). *The Pleasure of the Text*, trans. Richard Miller. New York: Hill & Wang.

Barthes, Roland (1977). *Image-Music-Text*, trans. Stephen Heath. New York: Hill & Wang.

Barthes, Roland (1977). *Roland Barthes by Roland Barthes*, trans. Richard Howard. New York: Hill & Wang.

Barthes, Roland (1982). *Empire of Signs*, trans. Richard Howard. New York: Hill & Wang.

Brooker, Peter (1999). *Cultural Theory: A Glossary.* London: Edward Arnold.

Lavers, Annette (1982). *Roland Barthes: Structuralism and After.* Cambridge, MA: Harvard University Press.

Zeman, J. Jay (1977). "Peirce's Theory of Signs." In *A Perfusion of Signs*, ed. Thomas A. Sebeok. Bloomington: Indiana University Press.

3. George Lakoff and Mark Johnson, *Metaphors We Live By*

Embler, Weller (1966). *Metaphor and Meaning.* DeLand, FL: Everett/Edwards.

Hayakawa, S. I. (1978). *Language and Thought in Action.* 4th edn. New York: Harcourt Brace Jovanovich.

Jakobsen, Roman (1988). "The Metaphoric and Metonymic Poles" in David Lodge, ed., *Modern Criticism and Theory: A Reader.* New York: Longman.

Kovecses, Zoltan. (2002). *Metaphor: A Practical Introduction.* Oxford: Oxford University Press.

Lakoff, George, and Mark Johnson (1980). *Metaphors We Live By.* Chicago: University of Chicago Press.

4. Aristotle, *Poetics*

Aristotle (2001). *Comedy*, trans. Arthur Asa Berger. New York: Xlibris.

Aristotle (1951). *Poetics*, trans. S. H. Butcher. In *The Great Critics*, ed. James Harry Smith and Edd Winfield Parks. 3rd edn. New York: W. W. Norton.

Certeau, Michel de (1984). *The practice of Everyday Life*, trans. Steven Randall. Berkeley: University of California Press.

Davis, Jessica Milner (2003). *Farce.* New Brunswick, NJ: Transaction.

Freud, Sigmund (1963). *Jokes and their Relation to the Unconscious*, trans. James Strachey. New York: W. W. Norton.

McKeon, R., ed. (1941). *The Basic Works of Aristotle.* New York: Random House.

Piddington, Ralph (1933). *The Psychology of Laughter.* London: Adelphi.

Tierno, Michael (2002). *Aristotle's Poetics for Screenwriters: Storytelling Secrets from the Greatest Mind in Western Civilization.* New York: Hyperion Press.

5. Tzvetan Todorov, *Introduction to Poetics*

Eagleton, Terry (1983). *Literary Theory: An Introduction.* Minneapolis: University of Minnesota Press.

Esslin, Martin (1982). *The Age of Television.* San Francisco: W. H. Freeman.

Todorov, Tzvetan (1973). *The Fantastic: A Structural Approach to a Literary Genre*, trans. Richard Howard. Cleveland, OH: Press of Case Western Reserve University.

Todorov, Tzvetan (1981). *Introduction to Poetics*, trans. Richard Howard. Minneapolis: University of Minnesota Press.

6. Vladimir Propp, *Morphology of the Folktale*

Bal, Mieke (1985). *Narratology: Introduction to the Theory of Narrative*, trans. C. van Boheemen. Toronto: University of Toronto Press.

Propp, Vladimir (1968). *Morphology of the Folktale*, trans. Laurence Scott. Austin: University of Texas Press.

Wright, Will (1975). *Sixguns and Society : A Structural Study of the Western*. Berkeley: University of California Press.

7. Janice Radway, *Reading the Romance*

Cassell, Justine, and Henry Jenkins, eds. (1999). *From Barbie to Mortal Kombat: Gender and Computer Games*. Cambridge, MA: The MIT Press.

Cortese, Anthony J. (1999). *Provocateur: Images of Women and Minorities in Advertising*. Lanham, MD: Rowman & Littlefield.

Helford, Elyce Rae, ed. (2000). *Fantasy Girls: Gender in the New Universe of Science Fiction and Fantasy Television*. Lanham, MD: Rowman & Littlefield.

Radway, Janice A. (1991). *Reading the romance: Women, Patriarchy, and Popular Literature*. Chapel Hill: University of North Carolina Press.

Surber, Jere Paul (1998). *Culture and Critique: An Introduction to the Critical Discourses of Cultural Studies*. Boulder, CO: Westview.

Wilcox, Rhonda V., and David Lavery, eds. (2002). *Fighting the Forces: What's at State in Buffy the Vampire Slayer*. Lanham, MD: Rowman & Littlefield.

8. Janet Murray, *Hamlet on the Holodeck*

Aarseth, Espen J. (1997). *Cybertext: Perspectives on Ergodic Literature*. Baltimore, MD: Johns Hopkins University Press.

Hertz, J. C. (1997). *Joystick Nation: How Videogames Ate Our Quarters, Won our Hearts and Rewired Our Minds*. Boston: Little, Brown.

Landow, George P. (1997). *Hypertext 2.0: The Convergence of Contemporary Critical Theory and Technology*. Baltimore, MD: Johns Hopkins University Press.

9. Mikhail Bakhtin, *The Dialogic Imagination*

Allen, Woody (1978). *Getting Even*. New York: Vintage.

Allen, Woody (1981). *Side Effects*. New York: Ballantine.

Bakhtin, Mikhail (1981). *The Dialogic Imagination: Four Essays*, trans. Caryl Emerson and Michael Holquist. Austin: University of Texas Press.

Bakhtin, Mikhail. (1984). *Rabelais and His World*, trans. Helene Iswolsky. Bloomington: Indiana University Press.

Dannow, D. K. (1991). *The Thought of Mikhail Bakhtin: From Word to Culture*. London: Macmillan.

Morris, Pam, ed. (1994). *The Bakhtin Reader: Selected Writings of Bakhtin, Medvedev, Voloshinov.* London: Edward Arnold.

10. Yuri Lotman, *Semiotics of Cinema*

Lotman, Jurij (1971). *The Structure of the Artistic Text,* trans. Gail Ienhoff and Ronald Vroon. Ann Arbor: Michigan Slavic Contributions.

Lotman, Jurij (1976). *Semiotics of Cinema,* trans. Mark E. Suino. Ann Arbor: Michigan Slavic Contributions.

Nichols, Mary P. (2000). *Reconstructing Woody: Art, Love, and Life in the Films of Woody Allen.* Lanham, MD: Rowman & Littlefield.

Shukman, Ann (1977). *Literature and Semiotics: A Study of the Writings of Yuri Lotman.* Amsterdam: North Holland.

Warshow, Robert (1970). *The Immediate Experience: Movies, Comics, Theater and Other Aspects of Popular Culture.* New York: Athaneum.

Wollen, Peter (1972). *Signs and Meaning in the Cinema.* Bloomington: University of Indiana Press.

11. Sergei Eisenstein, *Film Form*

De Nitto, Denis (1985). *Film, Form & Feeling.* New York: Harper and Row.

Denzin, Norman K. (1991). *Images of Postmodern Society: Social Theory and Contemporary Cinema.* Thousand Oaks, CA: Sage.

Eidsvik, Charles (1978). *Cineliteracy: Film Among the Arts.* New York: Random House.

Eisenstein, Sergei (1949). *Film Form: Essays in Film Theory,* trans. Jay Leyda. Bloomington: Indiana University Press.

Lehman, Peter, and William Luhr (2003). *Thinking About Movies: Watching, Questioning, Enjoying.* Oxford: Blackwell.

Monaco, James (2000). *How to Read a Film: The World of Movies, Media, Multimedia: Language, History, Theory.* 3rd edn. New York: Oxford University Press.

Wollen, Peter (1972). *Signs and Meaning in the Cinema.* Bloomington: Indiana University Press.

12. Raymond Williams, *Marxism and Literature*

Durham, Meenakshi Gigi, and Douglas M. Kellner, eds. (2001). *Media and Cultural Studies: Key Works.* Malden, MA: Blackwell.

Eagleton, Terry (1978). *Criticism and Ideology: A Study in Marxist Theory.* New York: W. W. Norton.

Higgins, John, ed. (2000). *The Raymond Williams Reader.* Oxford: Blackwell.

Tucker, Robert C., ed. (1972). *The Marx – Engels Reader.* New York: W. W. Norton.

Williams, Raymond (1958). *Culture and Society, 1780–1950.* London: Chatto and Windus.
Williams, Raymond (1977). *Marxism and Literature.* Oxford: Oxford University Press.

13. Henri Lefebvre, *Everyday Life in the Modern World*

Lefebvre, Henri (1971). *Everyday Life in the Modern World,* trans. Sacha Rabinovich. New York: Harper Torchbooks.
Solomon, Jack (1990). *The Signs of Our Times: The Secret Meanings of Everyday Life.* New York: Perennial.
Storey, John (1999). *Cultural Consumption and Everyday Life.* New York: Oxford University Press.

14. Michel de Certeau, *The Practice of Everyday Life*

Buchanan, Ian (2001). *Michel de Certeau: Cultural Theorist.* Thousand Oaks, CA: Sage.
Certeau, Michel de (1984). *The practice of Everyday Life,* trans. Steven Rendall. Berkeley: California University Press.
Certeau, Michel de (1986). *Heterologies: Discourse on the Other.* Minneapolis: University of Minnesota Press.
Gardiner, Michael (2000). *Critiques of Everyday Life: An Introduction.* New York: Routledge.
Stevenson, Nick (1985). *Understanding Media Cultures: Social Theory and Mass Communication.* London: Sage.

15. Marshall McLuhan, *Understanding Media*

McLuhan, Marshall (1951). *The Mechanical Bride: Folkore of Industrial Man.* New York: Vanguard. [Paperback edition, 1967. Boston: Beacon.]
McLuhan, Marshall (1962). *The Gutenberg Galaxy.* Toronto: University of Toronto Press.
McLuhan, Marshall (1965). *Understanding Media: The Extensions of Man.* New York: McGraw-Hill.
Theall, Donald F. (2001). *The Virtual Marshall McLuhan.* Montreal and Kingston: Queen's University Press.

16. Fredric Jameson, *Postmodernism, or, The Cultural Logic of Late Capitalism*

Berger, Arthur Asa, ed. (1998). *The Postmodern Presence: Readings on Postmodernism in American Culture and Society.* Walnut Creek, CA: AltaMira.

Best, Steven, and Douglas Kellner (1991). *Postmodern Theory: Critical Interrogations*. New York: Guilford.

Featherstone, Mike (1991). *Consumer Culture and Postmodernism*. London: Sage.

Gottdiener, Mark (1995). *Postmodern Semiotics: Material Culture and the Forms of Postmodern Life*. Cambridge, MA: Blackwell.

Hardt, Michael, and Kathi Weeks, eds. (2000). *The Jameson Reader*. Oxford: Blackwell.

Jameson, Fredric (1991). *Postmodernism, or, The Cultural Logic of Late Capitalism*. Durham, NC: Duke University Press.

Roberts, Adam (2000). *Fredric Jameson*. New York: Routledge.

17. Michael Thompson, Richard Ellis, Aaron Wildavsky, *Cultural Theory*

Chai, Sun-Ki, Brendon Swedlow, and Aaron B. Wildavsky, eds. (1998). *Cultural and Social Theory*. New Brunswick, NJ: Transaction.

Douglas, Mary (1975). *Implicit Meanings: Essays in Anthropology*. London: Routledge and Kegan Paul.

Falk, Pasi, and Colin Campbell, eds. (1997). *The Shopping Experience*. London: Sage.

Wildavsky, Aaron (1982). "Conditions for a Pluralist Democracy, or, Cultural Pluralism Means More Than One Political Culture in a Country." Unpublished manuscript.

18. bell hooks, *Black Looks: Race and Representation*

Berger, Arthur Asa (1974). *The Comic-stripped American*. New York: Walker.

Bobo, Jacqueline, ed. (2001). *Black Feminist Cultural Criticism*. Oxford: Blackwell.

Collins, Patricia Hill (1999). *Black Feminist Thought: Knowledge, Power, and the Politics of Empowerment*. New York: Routledge.

hooks, bell (1992). *Black Looks: Race and Representation*. Boston: South End Press.

Joyrich, Lynne (1996). *Re-Viewing Reception: Television, Gender, and Postmodern Culture*. Bloomington: Indiana University Press.

Schwichtenberg, Cathy, ed. (1993). *The Madonna Connection: Representational Politics, Subcultural Identities, and Cultural Theory*. Boulder, CO: Westview.

19. Stuart Hall, "The Work of Representation"

Hall, Stuart, ed. (1997). *Representation: Cultural Representations and Signifying Practices*. London: Sage.

Hoggart, Richard (1992). *The Uses of Literacy*. New Brunswick, NJ: Transaction.

hooks, bell (1994). *Outlaw Culture: Resisting Representations*. New York: Routledge.

Jensen, Joli (1990). *Redeeming Modernity: Contradictions in Media Criticism.* London: Sage.

Morley, Dave, and Kuan-Hsing Chen, eds. (1996). *Stuart Hall.* New York: Routledge.

Procter, James (2004). *Stuart Hall.* London: Routledge.

Rojek, Chris (2002). *Stuart Hall.* Cambridge: Polity.

Index

comedy
  laughter and liberation, 38–9
  why we laugh, 37–9
Comedy (Aristotle), 37
"Conditions for a Pluralist Democracy,
  or, Cultural Pluralism means More
  than One Political Culture in a
  Country" (Aaron Wildavsky), 148
Consumer Culture and Postmodernism
  (Mike Featherstone), 139–40
Course in General Linguistics (Ferdinand
  de Saussure), 9
*Cracking Jokes: Studies of Sick Humor
  Cycles* (Alan Dundes), 125
Crews, Frederick C., 58
criticism
  attack on autonomy of texts, 42
  focus on theory and not on texts, 43
Culler, Jonathan, 8
cultural theory
  grid-group typology, 149–50
  ways of life and media preferences,
  152–5
Cultural Theory: A Glossary (Peter
  Brooker), 16
Cultural Theory (Michael Thompson,
  Richard Ellis, Aaron Wildavsky),
  149–53
*Culture and Critique: An Introduction to
  Critical Discourses of Cultural
  Studies* (Jere Paul Surber), 56

DeNitto, Dennis, 96
dialogic, 75–6
  defined, 76
  importance of parody, 77–9
  intertextuality and creativity, 76–7
  theory of carnivalization, 75–6
Dialogic Imagination (M. M. Bakhtin),
  75–9
Don Quixote (Miguel Cervantes), 68
Doonesbury, 81
Douglas, Mary, 149, 170, 178

Dundes, Alan, 48, 49, 125
Durham, Meenakshi Gigi, 100
Durkheim, Émile, 4

Eidsvik, Charles, 92
Eisenstein, Sergei, 92–7
Elizabeth II, Queen 155
Ellis, Richard, 149–53
Embler, Weller, 24
Engels, Friedrich, 103
Esslin, Martin, 40
Evans, Dorothy, "Dot," 59
everyday life
  Certeau on strategies and tactics,
  122–3
  contrasted with the modern, 112
  defined, 111–12
  how consumers use media, 121–2
  "La Perruque," 123
  power of advertising in, 112–14
  power of festival in, 116
  semiotics and, 112–23
  terrorist societies and, 115–16
Everyday Life in the Modern World (Henri
  Lefebvre), 110–16, 121

Featherstone, Mike, 139
Ferdinand de Saussure (Jonathan Culler),
  8
Film, Form, & Feeling (Dennis DeNitto),
  96
Film Form: Essays in Film Theory (Sergei
  Eisenstein), 93–6
Financial Times (London) 134–7
  contrasted with *New York Times*, 136
  global perspective, 136
Freud, Sigmund, 38, 106, 171
Fry, William, 38

Gandhi, Mohandas, 155
"The Garden of Forking Paths" (Jorge
  Luis Borges), 65
Gehry, Frank, 142
